American Book Company
The Standards Experts

PASSING THE
GEORGIA 8TH GRADE CRCT
IN SCIENCE

Liz Thompson

American Book Company
PO Box 2638
Woodstock, GA 30188-1383
Toll Free: 1 (888) 264-5877   Phone: (770) 928-2834
Fax: (770) 928-7483 Toll Free Fax: 1 (866) 827-3240
Web site: www.americanbookcompany.com

ACKNOWLEDGEMENTS

The authors would like to gratefully acknowledge the formatting and technical contributions of Becky Wright.

We also want to thank Mary Stoddard for her expertise in developing the graphics for this book.

A special thanks to Marsha Torrens for her editing assistance.

This product/publication includes images from CorelDRAW 9 and 11 which are protected by the copyright laws of the United States, Canada and elsewhere. Used under license.

Table of Contents

Preface

The Georgia 8th Grade CRCT Test in Science will help students who are learning or reviewing material for the Georgia test that is now required for each gateway or benchmark course. **The materials in this book are based on the Georgia Performance Standards as published by the Georgia Department of Education**.

This book contains several sections. These sections are as follows: 1) General information about the book; 2) A Diagnostic Test and Evaluation Chart; 3) Domains/Chapters that teach the concepts and skills to improve readiness for Georgia 8th grade CRCT test in Science; 4) Two Post Tests. Answers to the tests and exercises are in a separate manual. The answer manual also contains a Chart of Standards for teachers to make a more precise diagnosis of student needs and assignments.

We welcome comments and suggestions about the book. Please contact us at

American Book Company **PO Box 2638** **Woodstock, GA 30188-1383**	**Toll Free: 1 (888) 264-5877** **Phone: (770) 928-2834** **Fax: (770) 928-7483** **Web site: www.americanbookcompany.com**

About the Author

Liz A. Thompson holds a B.S. in Chemistry and an M.S. in Analytical Chemistry, both from the Georgia Institute of Technology. Research conducted as both an undergraduate and graduate student focused on the creation and fabrication of sensors based on conducting polymers and biomolecules. Post graduate experience includes work in radioanalytical chemistry. Her publications include several articles in respected scientific journals, as well as authorship of two chapters in the textbook *Radioanalytical Chemistry* (2007). At every educational level, Mrs. Thompson has enjoyed teaching, tutoring and mentoring students in the study of science.

DIAGNOSTIC TEST

Diagnostic Test   **Answer Sheet**

Name: _____

Section 1

1. Ⓐ Ⓑ Ⓒ Ⓓ
2. Ⓐ Ⓑ Ⓒ Ⓓ
3. Ⓐ Ⓑ Ⓒ Ⓓ
4. Ⓐ Ⓑ Ⓒ Ⓓ
5. Ⓐ Ⓑ Ⓒ Ⓓ
6. Ⓐ Ⓑ Ⓒ Ⓓ
7. Ⓐ Ⓑ Ⓒ Ⓓ
8. Ⓐ Ⓑ Ⓒ Ⓓ
9. Ⓐ Ⓑ Ⓒ Ⓓ
10. Ⓐ Ⓑ Ⓒ Ⓓ
11. Ⓐ Ⓑ Ⓒ Ⓓ
12. Ⓐ Ⓑ Ⓒ Ⓓ
13. Ⓐ Ⓑ Ⓒ Ⓓ
14. Ⓐ Ⓑ Ⓒ Ⓓ
15. Ⓐ Ⓑ Ⓒ Ⓓ
16. Ⓐ Ⓑ Ⓒ Ⓓ
17. Ⓐ Ⓑ Ⓒ Ⓓ
18. Ⓐ Ⓑ Ⓒ Ⓓ
19. Ⓐ Ⓑ Ⓒ Ⓓ
20. Ⓐ Ⓑ Ⓒ Ⓓ
21. Ⓐ Ⓑ Ⓒ Ⓓ

22. Ⓐ Ⓑ Ⓒ Ⓓ
23. Ⓐ Ⓑ Ⓒ Ⓓ
24. Ⓐ Ⓑ Ⓒ Ⓓ
25. Ⓐ Ⓑ Ⓒ Ⓓ
26. Ⓐ Ⓑ Ⓒ Ⓓ
27. Ⓐ Ⓑ Ⓒ Ⓓ
28. Ⓐ Ⓑ Ⓒ Ⓓ
29. Ⓐ Ⓑ Ⓒ Ⓓ
30. Ⓐ Ⓑ Ⓒ Ⓓ

Section 2

31. Ⓐ Ⓑ Ⓒ Ⓓ
32. Ⓐ Ⓑ Ⓒ Ⓓ
33. Ⓐ Ⓑ Ⓒ Ⓓ
34. Ⓐ Ⓑ Ⓒ Ⓓ
35. Ⓐ Ⓑ Ⓒ Ⓓ
36. Ⓐ Ⓑ Ⓒ Ⓓ
37. Ⓐ Ⓑ Ⓒ Ⓓ
38. Ⓐ Ⓑ Ⓒ Ⓓ
39. Ⓐ Ⓑ Ⓒ Ⓓ
40. Ⓐ Ⓑ Ⓒ Ⓓ

41. Ⓐ Ⓑ Ⓒ Ⓓ
42. Ⓐ Ⓑ Ⓒ Ⓓ
43. Ⓐ Ⓑ Ⓒ Ⓓ
44. Ⓐ Ⓑ Ⓒ Ⓓ
45. Ⓐ Ⓑ Ⓒ Ⓓ
46. Ⓐ Ⓑ Ⓒ Ⓓ
47. Ⓐ Ⓑ Ⓒ Ⓓ
48. Ⓐ Ⓑ Ⓒ Ⓓ
49. Ⓐ Ⓑ Ⓒ Ⓓ
50. Ⓐ Ⓑ Ⓒ Ⓓ
51. Ⓐ Ⓑ Ⓒ Ⓓ
52. Ⓐ Ⓑ Ⓒ Ⓓ
53. Ⓐ Ⓑ Ⓒ Ⓓ
54. Ⓐ Ⓑ Ⓒ Ⓓ
55. Ⓐ Ⓑ Ⓒ Ⓓ
56. Ⓐ Ⓑ Ⓒ Ⓓ
57. Ⓐ Ⓑ Ⓒ Ⓓ
58. Ⓐ Ⓑ Ⓒ Ⓓ
59. Ⓐ Ⓑ Ⓒ Ⓓ
60. Ⓐ Ⓑ Ⓒ Ⓓ

SESSION 1

1 Aristide rows his raft across the river. S8P3b If he hits the dock head-on to stop, what will happen to the ball?

A. It will roll back toward Aristide.

B. It will roll forward toward the front of the raft.

C. It will roll sideways.

D. It will stop along with the raft.

2. The following diagram shows two sets S8P3c of hedge clippers. Which statement correctly describes the difference between them?

A  B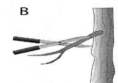

A. It will take less effort to chop at the branch with Clipper A than with Clipper B.

B. It will take less effort to chop at the branch with Clipper B than with Clipper A.

C. Both require the same amount of effort.

D. We need more information to decide which clipper requires more effort.

GO ON

3. In 1990, the discovery of the buckyball S8CS9 was announced. A buckyball is a ball- S8P1d shaped molecule consisting of 60 carbon atoms. Before the buckyball, only two forms of carbon were known: soft, black graphite and hard, transparent diamond. Which of the following hypotheses concerning the buckyball CANNOT be tested using scientific experimentation?

A. The buckyball is the most useful form of carbon.

B. The melting point of the buckyball is higher than the melting point of dia-mond.

C. The buckyball is harder than diamond.

D. The buckyball can be produced in the laboratory and can be found in nature.

4. You tear a tee shirt into small pieces and S8P1e then burn the pieces. Which of the following statements is correct?

A. Both actions are chemical changes.

B. Both actions are physical changes.

C. The first action is a physical change, and the second is a chemical change.

D. The first action is a chemical change, and the second is a physical change.

5. On the graph below, choose the line S8P3a which most closely describes the motion of a car between stop signs.

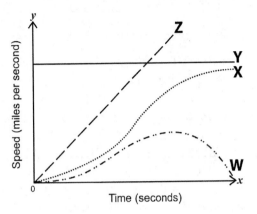

A. line W

B. line X

C. line Y

D. line Z

6. Which of the following correctly S8P2c describes the energetic transition that takes place when you turn on a light bulb?

A. Turning on a light bulb is the conversion of electrical energy to electromagnetic energy.

B. Turning on a light bulb creates thermal energy from chemical energy.

C. Turning on a light bulb creates electrical energy from electromagnetic energy.

D. Turning on a light bulb is the conversion of electrical energy to chemical energy.

GO ON

Use this data table to answer question 7.

	Initial Density (grams/cm^3)	Food Color added (mL)	Final Density (grams/cm^3)	Final Color
Sample A	1.0	1	1.1	orange
Sample B	1.0	5	1.2	orange
Sample C	1.0	7	1.2	blue

7. Reese's teacher gave her three [S8P1d, 1e, S8CS7d] test tubes, each containing an unknown liquid sample of a given density. Reese added orange food coloring to each test tube and then calculated the density of the sample. She placed the data she collected in the data table. She concluded that the added food color increased the density of the sample. What is another reasonable interpretation of this data?

A. Sample A is a different substance than Sample B.

B. Sample C is a different substance than Samples A or B.

C. All three samples contain water.

D. None of the samples contains water.

GO ON

Answer questions 8 – 9 based on the summary of the following experiment.

A group of students investigated how temperature affects the rate of chemical reactions. They used hydrogen peroxide, which breaks down into oxygen and water, for their experiment. The students measured how long it took to obtain 50 mL of oxygen gas from a given volume of hydrogen peroxide heated to different temperatures. Their data are shown in the table below.

Temperature (°C)	Time (minutes)
10	33
20	16
30	8
40	4
50	2

8. Based on the students' data, select the correct conclusion about the rate of this chemical reaction.   S8CS7b

   A. Reaction rates increase as time increases.

   B. Reaction rates decrease as time decreases.

   C. Reaction rates increase as temperature increases.

   D. Reaction rates decrease as temperature increases.

9. Select the best way for the students to reduce the experimental error in their investigation.   S8CS9c, e

   A. test more than one variable at a time

   B. perform repeated trials

   C. change their answers if they do not match their hypothesis

   D. perform the experiment only one time

10. The diagram of a wave indicates two important properties of a wave: its wavelength and amplitude. Wavelength is inversely related to frequency: a longer wavelength indicates a lower frequency. Amplitude is proportional to the intensity of the energy that the wave can impart to matter: a greater amplitude indicates a greater intensity. Consider the following situation: Wave A has a wavelength 5λ and an amplitude 2γ, while Wave B has a wavelength 3λ and an amplitude 4γ. Which statement best describes these two waves?   S8P4f

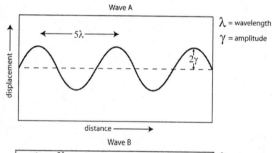

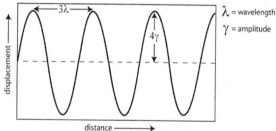

A. Wave A has a lower frequency and greater intensity than Wave B.

B. Wave A has a higher frequency and greater intensity than Wave B.

C. Wave A has a higher frequency and lower intensity than Wave B.

D. Wave A has a lower frequency and lower intensity than Wave B.

11. Use the diagram below to tell where the most reactive metals are located.   S8P1f

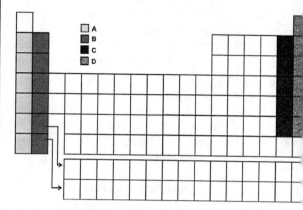

A. light gray, section A

B. dark gray, section B

C. black, section C

D. textured, section D

12. Select the observation that does NOT support the conclusion that a chemical reaction took place.   S8P1e

A. Liquid water changed to water vapor.

B. A precipitate was formed.

C. An odor developed.

D. Temperature rose.

13. An example of using a lever is   S8P3c

A. using a big spoon to stir a pot of soup.

B. using a fork to scramble an egg.

C. using a ramp to roll a barrel into a pickup truck.

D. using a screwdriver to pry the lid off a can of paint.

 GO ON

14. As illustrated in the diagram below, Carl S8P1g investigated the change of mass during a chemical reaction. He massed a plastic bottle that contained 50 mL of water, a balloon and two seltzer tablets. He recorded a total mass of 200g. Carl put the seltzer tablets inside the balloon and pulled the balloon over the neck of the bottle. He shook the balloon so the seltzer tablets fell into the water. Carl observed the tablets fizzing and the balloon expanding. Carl again massed his apparatus, after the fizzing and the expansion of the balloon stopped.

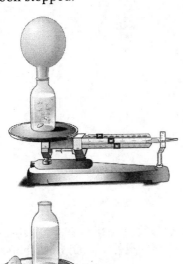

If the combined mass of the two seltzer tablets before they were dropped into the water was 5 g, select the mass of Carl's apparatus at the end of his investigation.

A. 195 g

B. between 195 g and 200 g

C. 200 g

D. more than 200 g

Use the following figure to answer question 15.

15. Which of the following is the best S8CS3d measurement of volume on this graduated cylinder?

A. 5.7 mL

B. 5.6 mL

C. 5.55 mL

D. 5.65 mL

16. Think of the threading of a screw being   S8P3c
unwrapped, as in the following figure. Which
statement correctly describes the simple
machine represented in the screw?

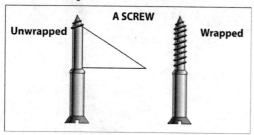

A SCREW

Unwrapped   Wrapped

A. The thread of a screw is a wedge wrapped
   around a shaft.

B. The thread of a screw is an inclined plane
   wrapped around a shaft.

C. The thread of a screw is a lever wrapped
   around a shaft.

D. The thread of a screw is a pulley
   wrapped around a shaft.

17. The following figure describes the   S8P1c
molecular motion of a sample of matter.
Which of the following can you conclude is
NOT the identity of the sample?

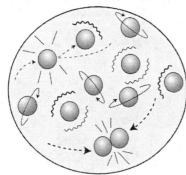

A. hydrogen gas

B. iron ore

C. superheated steam

D. liquid nitrogen

18. In the following concept map, some   S8P1d
items are missing. Which of the following is
NOT an item that could appear as a physical
property?

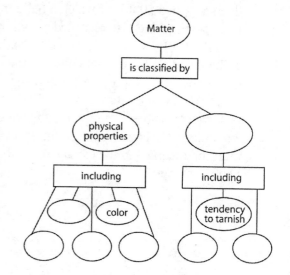

A. smell

B. flammability

C. shape

D. taste

19. Select the situation that will result in the   S8P5a
greatest gravitational force between two
bodies.

A. large combined mass and small distance
   apart

B. large combined mass and great distance
   apart

C. small combined mass and great distance
   apart

D. small combined mass and small distance
   apart

GO O

Use the data table to answer questions 20 and 21.

Measurer	Length (m)	Method
Julie	1.67	Tape measure
Tiffany	1.68	Meter stick
Scott	1.67	Tape measure
Andrew	1.8	Caliper

20. Four friends independently measured   S8CS4b
the length of a lever's resistance arm. Julie
and Scott chose to use a 4-meter long tape
measure. They were both able to complete
the measurement without moving the tape
measure. Tiffany chose a meter stick, which
she had to move once to complete the
measurement. Andrew chose to use a 3-
centimeter caliper, which he had to move 60
times before he completed the measurement.
Their measurements are shown in the data
table. Which method is the best, and why?

   A. Andrew's method was the best, because the
   caliper is a very precise measurement tool.

   B. Julie and Scott's method was best
   because it produced the most consistent
   results.

   C. Tiffany's method was best, because her
   data closely matched Julie and Scott's
   data.

   D. Julie's method was best because she
   thought of it before Scott.

21. Julie put a bookbag on the resistance   S8P3c
arm of the lever. What would you do to
decrease the work input needed to lift the
bookbag with the lever?

   A. Move the fulcrum closer to the bookbag.

   B. Move the fulcrum farther away from the
   bookbag.

   C. Remove books from the bookbag.

   D. Both A and C will decrease the work
   input.

Use the figure to answer questions 22 and 23.

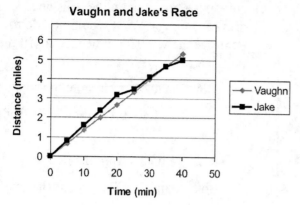

Vaughn and Jake's Race

22. Predict when Vaughn will cross the finish line. S8CS6c

   A. at the 40-minute mark

   B. between 45 and 50 minutes

   C. at the fifty-minute mark

   D. at sometime beyond 50 minutes

23. At what time (t) does Vaughn experience negative acceleration? S8P3a

   A. at t = 0

   B. between t=20 and t=30

   C. at t = 45

   D. Vaughn does not experience any deceleration during the race.

24. Walt would like a glass of orange juice. Which unit would be appropriate to measure the volume of juice he pours? S8CS3c,d

   A. milligrams

   B. grams

   C. milliliters

   D. liters

25. A bar magnet is a permanent magnet, and is surrounded by magnetic field lines. Describe the direction of its magnetic field lines. S8P5c

   A. from the north pole of the magnet to its south pole

   B. from the south pole of the magnet to its north pole

   C. upwards from a central point between the poles

   D. directly outwards from the south pole

26. Which of the following situations would ALWAYS result in no electrical current flow? S8P5b

   A. an open switch in a parallel circuit

   B. an open switch in a series circuit

   C. three resistors in a series circuit

   D. adding a resistor to a parallel circuit

GO ON

27. A biologist uses a laser beam to identify the organism that he wants his photographer to take a picture of. He shines the laser at the surface of shallow water on a calm day. Which organisms will be illuminated by the light?   S8P4b

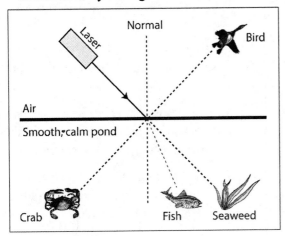

A. the crab and the fish

B. the fish and the bird

C. the crab and the bird

D. the seaweed and the bird

28. Which of the following scenarios would result in the loudest sound being heard?   S8P4d

A. Two asteroids collide in space.

B. Two rocks are struck against each other underwater.

C. Two rocks are struck against each other in humid air.

D. Two rocks are struck against each other in dry air.

29. A power plant generates thermal energy, which is often used to heat water. Steam from the hot water then turns turbines, which generate electricity. The steam then cools and condenses into liquid water. At which stage do the water molecules have the most kinetic energy?   S8P1c

A. when they are present as hot water

B. when they are present as cool water

C. when they are in gaseous form

D. when they are condensing

30. Density is measured in which of the following units?   S8P1d

A. grams per milliliter

B. milliliters per gram

C. grams per millimeter

D. newtons

SESSION 2

31. Which of the following statements describes sunlight? S8P4a

    A. Sunlight consists of colorless electromagnetic waves.

    B. Sunlight is composed of only visible electromagnetic waves.

    C. Sunlight is composed of only visible and ultraviolet electromagnetic waves.

    D. Sunlight is composed of all wavelengths of the electromagnetic spectrum.

32. Mike and Don both hit a baseball. Don hits the ball harder. The crack of the bat is much louder when Don hits the ball than when Mike does. Which characteristic of the sound waves produced results in Don's hit being louder? S8P4a,e

    A. increased amplitude

    B. increased frequency

    C. increased diffraction

    D. increased pitch

33. Why do electrical workers often wear rubber boots and gloves? S8P5c

    A. Because rubber is a thermal insulator.

    B. Because rubber is an electrical insulator.

    C. Because rubber is a thermal conductor.

    D. Because rubber is an electrical conductor.

34. Mara has a glass beaker of water with a thermometer in it. At time t=0 minutes, the thermometer reads 17° C. At time t=40 minutes, the thermometer reads 25° C. Which statement correctly describes this scenario? S8P2d

    A. The temperature of the water increased because it transferred energy to the surrounding air.

    B. The temperature of the water increased because the surrounding air transferred thermal energy to the water.

    C. The temperature of the water increased because the thermal energy of the water and air were equivalent.

    D. The temperature of the water increased because glass is a thermal insulator.

12

35. Examine the following diagram. An increase in pitch is a result of which of the following? S8P4f

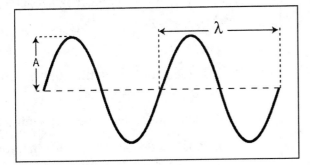

A. increased A

B. decreased A

C. increased λ

D. decreased λ

36. Which of the following action would result in a chemical reaction? S8P1e

A. mixing liquid water with solid salt

B. mixing liquid water with liquid oil

C. mixing solid salt with liquid motor oil

D. mixing solid salt with liquid ammonia.

37. Susan performs a laboratory experiment that includes a strongly exothermic chemical reaction. Which of the following pieces of safety equipment is unnecessary? S8CS2a

A. safety goggles

B. gloves

C. lab coat or smock

D. earplugs

38. Which is an example of kinetic energy? S8P2b

A. an apple

B. a light bulb

C. an ocean wave

D. a battery

39. Your mom looks in the rearview mirror of the car to check the position of other cars nearby. What behavior of light allows her to see the cars in the mirror? S8P4b,c

A. reflection

B. refraction

C. diffraction

D. radiation

40. A chemical property of an acid would be S8P1d

A. sour taste.

B. electrical conductivity.

C. bitter taste.

D. high pH.

41. A linen curtain allows light to pass through but diffuses it. The curtain may be described as S8P4b

A. opaque.

B. translucent.

C. transparent.

D. insulating.

42. Pressing on the brake pedal of a car   S8P3b
causes a brake pad to be applied to a rotor. This application of pressure slows the rotation of the wheel, resulting in a decrease in speed of the car. What force slows the rotation of the wheel?

   A. friction

   B. nuclear

   C. gravitational

   D. electromagnetic

43. Describe what is happening in the   S8P1e
following figure.

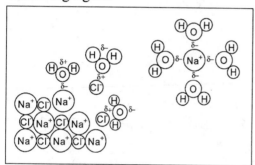

   A. A sample of NaCl is chemically reacting with water to form a new compound.

   B. A sample of NaCl is physically mixing with water to form a solution.

   C. A sample of NaCl is physically mixing with water to form an acid.

   D. A sample of NaCl is physically mixing with water to form a base.

44. Which of the following is not a group   S8P1f
on the Periodic Table?

   A. halogens

   B. alkali soil metals

   C. noble gases

   D. actinides

45. Absolute zero is at 0K, or -273.15° C. It   S8P2d
is possible to cool laboratory samples to near absolute zero, but absolute zero has not yet been reached by scientists. If scientists were to cool a laboratory sample to absolute zero, what would happen?

   A. The sample would combust.

   B. All atomic motion in the sample would cease.

   C. Atomic motion would be at a minimum.

   D. Electrical conductivity of the sample would decrease to a minimum.

46. Talia ran the 100 meter dash at her   S8P3a
school's track and field meet. Her average velocity over the course of the race was 15 m/s. How long did it take her to complete the race?

   A. less than 5 seconds

   B. between 5 and 6 seconds

   C. between 6 and 7 seconds

   D. over 7 seconds

47. Examine the following diagram.   S8P3b
Describe the motion of the trunk.

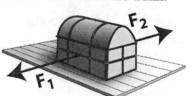

   A. The trunk will move to the left.

   B. The trunk will move to the right.

   C. The trunk will not move.

   D. We cannot know how the trunk will move without knowing the magnitude of the forces.

GO ON

48. Which of the following is an element? S8P1a,b

    A. carbon dioxide

    B. phosphorous

    C. water

    D. ammonia

49. An electric circuit allows electricity to S8P5c
flow between two poles: a negative pole and
a positive pole. What is present in excess at
the negative pole?

    A. protons

    B. neutrons

    C. electrons

    D. atoms

50. A sample of water vapor condenses to S8P2d
form liquid water. What change in water
allows this to happen?

    A. Water molecules get closer together.

    B. Water molecules get farther apart.

    C. Water molecules increase in size.

    D. Oxygen and hydrogen atoms decrease in
size.

51. Which phase of matter has both a S8P1c
defined volume and a defined shape?

    A. solid

    B. liquid

    C. gas

    D. plasma

**Use the following table to answer questions
52 and 53.**

Element	Density	Phase at 25°C
lead (Pb)	11.3 g/cm^3	solid
bromine (Br)	3.1 g/cm^3	liquid
manganese (Mn)	7.2 g/cm^3	solid
sodium (Na)	0.97 g/cm^3	solid
silicon(Si)	2.33 g/cm^3	solid

52. Blocks of each material in the table S8P1d
were formed, each with a volume of 10 cm^3.
Which block was the heaviest?

    A. Pb

    B. Br

    C. Mn

    D. Na

53. Which of the materials required a S8P1c
container to conform to a 10 cm^3 block?

    A. Pb

    B. Br

    C. Na

    D. Si

54. Sound is created by S8P4d, e

    A. gravity.

    B. frictional forces.

    C. vibrating matter.

    D. exothermic reactions.

55. The diagram below suggests that at   S8P4b
dawn the sun appears higher in the sky than it
actually is. Which property of light explains
this phenomenon?

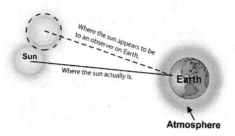

A. absorption

B. diffraction

C. reflection

D. refraction

56. Which of the following cannot be found   S8P1f
on the Periodic Table?

A. aluminum chloride

B. nitrogen

C. titanium

D. magnesium

Use the data table to answer question 57.

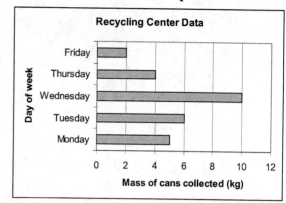

57. A local recycling center collected   S8CS3b
aluminum cans throughout a week, as
described in the data table. On what day of
the week was the median data point found?

A. Monday

B. Tuesday

C. Wednesday

D. Friday

58. Lupe conducts an experiment to see   S8P2a
how much electricity she can generate by
pedaling a bicycle hooked up to a generator.
At the end of the experiment, she calculates
that she did 500 joules of work but only
produced 400 joules of energy in the form of
electricity. Where did the other 100 joules
go?

A. It was destroyed by the friction of the bike.

B. Friction between the parts of the bike
lowered energy output.

C. The rubber wheels of the bike block
some of the electricity.

D. It was recycled back into the bike
generator.

59. The wavelength of blue light is   S8P4c
around 475 nanometers. A blue sky
appears blue because it

    A. absorbs light with a wavelength of 475 nm.

    B. reflects all visible light except light with
    a wavelength of 475 nm.

    C. reflects only visible light with a wave-
    length of 475 nm.

    D. reflects only ultraviolet light.

60. Savannah adds 25 mg of KCl to 50 mL   S8P1d
of water. Which of the following will result?

    A. A chemical reaction will occur.

    B. A solution will form which has a lower
    density than water.

    C. A solution will form which has a higher
    density than water.

    D. A precipitate will form.

STOP

EVALUATION CHART

GEORGIA 8TH GRADE CRCT IN SCIENCE
DIAGNOSTIC TEST

Directions: On the following chart, circle the question numbers that you answered incorrectly, and evaluate the results. Then turn to the appropriate topics (listed by chapters), read the explanations, and complete the exercises. Review other chapters as needed. Finally, complete the Post Tests to prepare for the Georgia 8th Grade CRCT in Science.

Chapters	Question Numbers
Chapter 1: What is Science?	7, 9
Chapter 2: The Basic Method	3
Chapter 3: Equipment and Measurement	15, 20, 24
Chapter 4: Data and Its Presentation	22, 57
Chapter 5: Laboratory Safety	37
Chapter 6: Atoms and Elements	11, 44, 48, 56
Chapter 7: Properties of Matter	3, 4, 7, 12, 18, 30, 36, 40, 43, 48, 52, 60
Chapter 8: Chemical Reactions	14
Chapter 9: States of Matter	17, 29, 51
Chapter 10: Energy	6, 38, 58
Chapter 11: Thermal Energy	34, 45, 50
Chapter 12: Velocity and Acceleration	5, 23, 46
Chapter13: Forces and Motion	1, 19, 42, 47
Chapter 14: Work	2, 13, 16, 21
Chapter 15:Electromagnetic Force	25, 33, 49

Chapters	Question Numbers
Chapter 16: Electrical Circuits	26
Chapter 17: Electricity in our Lives	6, 26, 58
Chapter 18: Properties of Waves	10, 28, 31, 32, 35, 54
Chapter 19: Behavior of Waves	27, 32, 39, 41, 55, 59

Unit 1
Characteristics of Science

The chapters in this Unit cover the following standards:

Chapter 1:

S8CS1a: Understand the importance of —and keep—honest, clear and accurate records in science.

S8CS7a: Question claims based on vague attributions (such as "leading doctors say...") or on statements made by people outside the area of their particular expertise.

S8CS7b: Identify the flows of reasoning in arguments that are based on poorly designed research (e.g., facts intermingled with opinion, conclusions based on insufficient evidence).

S8CS7c: Question the value of arguments based on small samples of data, biased samples or samples for which there was no control.

S8CS7d: Recognize that there may be more than one way to interpret a given set of findings.

S8CS9d: Scientist often collaborate to design research. To prevent this bias, scientists conduct independent studies of the same questions.

S8CS9e: Accurate record keeping, data sharing and replication of results are essential for maintaining an investigator's credibility with other scientists and society.

S8CS9g: The ethics of science require that special care must be taken and used for human subjects and animals in scientific research. Scientists must adhere to the appropriate rules and guidelines when conducting research.

Chapter 2:

S8CS1b: Understand that hypotheses can be valuable even if they turn out not to be completely accurate.

S8CS6a: Write clear, step-by-step instructions for conducting scientific investigations, operating a piece of equipment or following a procedure.

S8CS9a: Investigations are conducted for different reasons, which include exploring new phenomena, confirming previous results, testing how well a theory predicts and comparing different theories. Scientific investigations usually involve collecting evidence, reasoning, devising hypotheses and formulating explanations to make sense of collected evidence.

S8CS9b: Scientific investigations usually involve collecting evidence, reasoning, devising hypotheses and formulating explanations to make sense of collected evidence.

S8CS9c: Scientific experiments investigate the effect of one variable on another. All other variables are kept constant.

Chapter 3:

S8CS3a: Analyze scientific data by using, interpreting and comparing numbers in several equivalent forms, such as integers, fractions, decimals and percents.

S8CS3c: Apply the metric system to scientific investigations that include metric to metric conversion (i.e., centimeters to meters.)

S8CS3d: Decide what degree of precision is adequate and round off appropriately.

S8CS3e: Address the relationship between accuracy and precision.

S8CS3f: Use ratios and proportions, including constant rates, in appropriate problems.

S8CS4b: Use appropriate tools and units for measuring objects and/or substances.

S8CS9f: Scientists use technology and mathematics to enhance the process of scientific inquiry.

Chapter 4:

S8CS3b: Find the mean, median and mode and use them to analyze a set of scientific data.

S8CS4a: Use appropriate technology to store and retrieve scientific information in topical, alphabetical, numerical and keyword files, and create simple files.

S8CS5a: Observe and explain how parts can be related to other parts in a system such as the role of simple machines in complex machines.

S8CS5b: Understand that different models (such as physical replicas, pictures, and analogies) can be used to represent the same thing.

S8CS6b: Write for scientific purposes incorporating information from a circle, bar, or line graph, data tables, diagrams and symbols.

S8CS6c: Organize scientific information in appropriate tables, charts, and graphs and identify relationships they reveal.

Chapter 5:

S8CS2a: Follow correct procedures for use of scientific apparatus.

S8CS2b: Demonstrate appropriate techniques in all laboratory situations.

S8CS2c: Follow correct protocol for identifying and reporting safety problems and violations.

S8CS4c: Learn and use standard safety practices when conducting scientific investigations.

SCIENCE

8th Grade CRCT

Chapter 1
What is Science?

What is Science?

That is a pretty big question. In order to help you think it through, the first few chapters of this book will examine the rules and processes of science; however, let's first look at what science is **not**.

Science is not:

- an expression of our own personal beliefs.

- an argument that favors only one position.

- showing off that you are smart (or not) to other people.

- a set of random facts to memorize.

OK, so what is it? When you think of the word **science**, you probably think of microscopes and atoms, theories and equations...you might even think of old scientists that you have seen in black and white pictures from your textbooks.

All of those things are certainly aspects of science, but it is so much more. Science is the process by which humans question, investigate, explore, invent and improve the world around us. That is a powerful set of activities. The process can lead to great advancements in both our lives and in our environment. Such a powerful process must have some rules that govern it, right? In fact, there are rules. The rules take the form of a set of standard practices that scientists are expected to follow. The point is to separate "good"

Figure 1.1 Aspects of Science

science from "bad" science. Good science is based on ethical principles and has been reviewed by fellow scientists. Bad science is based on immoral principles or is unsupported by established data or methods. The scientific community decides what is "good" and what is "bad" through the disciplined practice of communication.

MODES OF SCIENTIFIC COMMUNICATION

Scientists communicate to share ideas and to gain new perspectives. Communicating scientific discoveries provides knowledge to others in the scientific community. It allows other scientists to confirm or disagree with the work of their colleagues. The process makes knowledge available so that it can be applied to different problems. This expanded research can lead to new discoveries.

Figure 1.2

One way of communicating a scientific discovery is through a journal article. A **journal** is a specialized publication. There are thousands of scientific journals, focusing on a wide variety of subject areas. *Science* and *Nature* are two widely-read journals. Other journals, like *Analytical Chemistry* or *Environmental Science and Technology* focus on a narrower range of topics.

The papers published in a journal undergo peer review. **Peer review** is the process of making sure everything is correct in both the methods and conclusions of an article. Peer review is performed by scientists in a similar field. They look carefully at every detail of the experiment to make sure the experiment was conducted using a sound scientific method. If the peer-review committee accepts the paper, it usually gets published.

Once the scientific community has shared information, the general public is next to learn about new discoveries. The media and health agencies provide the information to the public, and textbooks and teachers communicate the information to students. Publications like *Scientific American* and *Discover* are great for keeping up-to-date on scientific progress without delving into the journals. These **magazines** are factual and reliable but not peer reviewed (so they are not called journals).

Information is also found on the Internet. But beware! This information can be fact, opinion or even lies — and you must learn to tell the difference. One clue is in the Web address's suffix. A .gov suffix is a government Web site, .org is an organization and can be almost anyone! Another suffix is .edu, which is a college or university Web site. Think about the information you are looking for and decide which type of site will be the most reliable.

ETHICAL PRACTICES

It is very important that you understand the "rules of the road" for ethical behavior, both as a member of society and as a scientist carrying out research. What are ethics? **Ethics** are a set of beliefs and behaviors that emphasize moral duty and social obligation. More basically, it is the knowledge of right and wrong and the ability to behave accordingly. Ethics in science can be separated into two basic groups: **appropriate subjects of research** and **integrity of scientific methods**.

APPROPRIATE SUBJECTS OF RESEARCH

Sometimes people question whether scientific research is a good thing or bad thing. This is especially true in biological fields or fields in which testing is done on humans or animals. Scientific ethics also come into play when the results or processes of an experiment conflict with the beliefs of some group of people. The conflict may be a religious one, as in the debate over the teaching of evolution or stem cell research. It may be an environmental conflict, as in the debate over global warming. It may be a conflict in Congress, as in the yearly debate over which scientific discipline should get more government funding.

Figure 1.3 Consensus

In all these cases, questioning and debating should NOT be considered a "bad" thing. Carefully considering the impact of a certain line of scientific inquiry is a VERY worthwhile and productive discussion. The point is to reach a **consensus** (agreement) of opinion on which investigations will do the most good and the least harm, while also taking into account how much they will cost and whether the cost is justified. The point is not for one side to "win."

Figure 1.4 No Consensus

INTEGRITY OF SCIENTIFIC METHODS

The way that scientists carry out an experiment is called the **scientific method**. This, too, has an ethical component. For example, it would be highly unethical for a scientist to claim a new drug works when it really doesn't. The method must be described completely so that other scientists can follow the same procedure. The data must be reported truthfully so that other scientists can verify it. If other scientists cannot duplicate the published results, the whole experiment is in question.

There is much more to being a scientist than knowing facts and investigation methods. Being a scientist places you in a group of people who value truth and accuracy.

But with all the scientific claims you see every day, it may be sometimes difficult to tell the difference between science and sales. You can probably think of at least one situation where scientific research has been used to support one product or another. How do you know the information you see is true and correct?

One way is through the results of a **clinical trial**. This is a kind of experiment where products (particularly medicines) are tested on animals or people. A clinical trial only occurs after the product has been well-researched and tested in the laboratory. The results of the trial are data that help the makers of the product decide if the product can be sold to the public. Often, these results are used in the advertisements that you see every day.

Figure 1.5 Advertisements

Sometimes no scientific results appear to be available. What do you believe then? Well, you may be thinking that you will just accept the advertisement or claim as it is.

Who would want to publish false information anyway?

Well, scientific research is often connected with **economic** (concerning money) or **political** (concerning government or laws) issues. These issues can influence the scientists performing the research by causing **bias** in their interpretation of the data. Biased data has been interpreted to suit the goals of the interpreter. Let's look at two situations that involve bias.

Figure 1.6 Ghost Activity

UNINTENTIONAL BIAS

People usually pay more attention to data that confirms their beliefs. If you believe in ghosts, you are more likely to interpret mysterious sights or sounds as GHOST ACTIVITY! Someone who does not believe in ghosts would probably interpret a ghostly figure in the corner as the work of a pesky sister. *This kind of bias is unintentional.*

INTENTIONAL BIAS

People may give more weight to data that will give them a reward. If good clinical trial results for a new acne treatment will advance the career of the researchers involved, they may be more likely to overlook the fact that the medicines make some of the study participants feel sick, sprout white nose hair or have bad skin reactions. *This kind of bias may be intentional.*

Figure 1.7 Acne Treatment

Is bias the only reason that false information is published?

When a few different researchers all interpret the data differently, bias could be a factor. On the other hand, sometimes people just naturally look at things in different ways. It could also be that the experiment was poorly designed, giving unclear data.

There is a final complicating factor that is exceptionally important to consider. There might be factors affecting the experiment that are not known, despite the best efforts of scientists. In the next chapter, we will examine experimental methods to hopefully avoid as many errors and unknowns as possible.

SCIENCE, TECHNOLOGY AND SOCIETY

Society (people like you) impacts technology by deciding what type of technology is useful and acceptable. However, not all societies come to the same conclusions.

For example, some countries, like France, use nuclear power plants to generate the majority of their electricity. In other countries, like Austria and Ireland, the public opinion is that nuclear technologies are too dangerous and should not be used at all. In the United States, about 20% of our electricity comes from nuclear power plants. Each of these societies has reached a different consensus.

Consider this: for every technological advancement made, there are drawbacks to consider. For example, wind power is a renewable source of energy. However, the windmills used to harness this power source take up a great deal of space and are unattractive to look at and listen to. Wind power is also more expensive than power generated by nuclear and fossil fuel plants. Raising power costs would affect many people, including people who cannot afford the increase. Try to think of each individual technology in terms of risks and benefits. It's called a **risk-benefit analysis**. It means to investigate if the risk of doing something is outweighed by the benefit of doing it. A favorable risk-benefit analysis results when the benefits outweigh the risks.

Figure 1.8
Weighing Risks and Benefits

Whatever the topic, a thorough risk-benefit analysis requires a lot of research and discussion to complete. Careful use of journals, magazines and the Internet are a good start. Thoughtful discussions with your parents, friends, teachers and experts on the subject are also important. No matter how formal you make your investigation, the ability to think of issues in terms of risk and benefit is an important life skill that will help you make decisions and become a thoughtful, contributing member of society. It will also help you understand why ethical practices are sometimes difficult to define.

CHAPTER 1 REVIEW

1. A vital part of growing up is the development of your sense of ethical behavior. Which of the following activities will have the **least** impact on this development?

   A. discussing events at school with your parents and friends
   B. playing sports or engaging in competitions and debate
   C. going shopping at the mall or going out to eat
   D. reading the newspaper or novels about other cultures

2. One component of ethical behavior is social obligation. Which of the following activities **does not** display a sense of social obligation?

   A. graduating from high school
   B. developing strong and healthy friendships
   C. littering and vandalism
   D. conserving energy and reducing waste

3. Which of the following is **not** a component of "good" science?

   A. It is ethical in nature.
   B. It is reviewed and accepted by peer scientists.
   C. It is carried out using secret methods.
   D. It is reproducible.

4. Which of the following is **most likely** to be a peer-reviewed journal?

   A. *National Geographic*   C. *Scientific American*
   B. *New England Journal of Medicine*   D. *Ladies' Home Journal*

5. Which of the following activities is **most** important in deciding whether or not an investigation is an appropriate subject of research?

   A. performing a poll to determine what others think of the research
   B. attending public forums and scientific conferences to discuss and debate the risks and benefits of the research
   C. figuring out how much money can be made if the research results in a new drug or product
   D. asking a non-profit or government agency what type of research would benefit its program

1.	Ⓐ	Ⓑ	Ⓒ	Ⓓ
2.	Ⓐ	Ⓑ	Ⓒ	Ⓓ
3.	Ⓐ	Ⓑ	Ⓒ	Ⓓ
4.	Ⓐ	Ⓑ	Ⓒ	Ⓓ
5.	Ⓐ	Ⓑ	Ⓒ	Ⓓ

Chapter 2
The Basic Method

In Chapter 1, we discussed the place of science in society. Now, it is time to look at how the process of science is conducted. The Latin root for the word "science" is *scientia*, meaning knowledge. Through science, we design and carry out experiments to gain more knowledge of natural phenomena in the universe around us.

A SCIENTIFIC PROCESS

Are you a scientist? You may not think so, but you have been one since you were very young. Need proof? Good. A real scientist would never blindly accept someone else's conclusion without seeing some **data** (supporting evidence)! Now let's revisit a scene from your early childhood to find some of that supporting evidence.

Let's see, how about the first time you threw a ball down and noticed that it bounced back up from the ground? You probably threw the ball harder and harder, and noticed that it bounced back up higher and higher. This may not have seemed like serious science inquiry to you. You may not have known all the science terminology (words) that went along with it, but it most definitely WAS science. Here, in a nutshell, is the scientific process you went through.

Before you threw the ball to the ground you had a **question** in mind:

What will happen if I throw my ball down to the ground?

Figure 2.1 Throwing Balls

So you did some **research**. Research brings to mind a lot of reading in the library, but research is actually any activity that generates supporting evidence. We talked about some methods of research in Chapter 1, but there are others. In this case, you were still a tiny person who couldn't read, talk or use a computer yet. So your research was to **observe** (or watch) other kids throwing balls. When those balls bounced back you asked:

Does this bouncing thing work for MY ball?

So, you threw the ball to the ground and found out that it did bounce. Cool...but this made you ask more questions. Scientific thoughts whirred around in your head. Maybe one was:

What happens if I throw the ball harder? Softer?

Figure 2.2 Boy Bouncing a Ball

Based on what you saw other kids do, you THOUGHT the ball should go higher when you threw it harder toward the ground, but you wanted to KNOW this was so. At this point, you had a working **hypothesis**. A hypothesis is a statement that predicts the relationship between two variables in an experiment. To test your hypothesis, you threw the ball.

Even though you may not have put it in these terms, when you threw the ball with increasing amounts of force, you were trying to figure out the relationship between how hard you threw the ball and the responding height of the bounces. To put it another way, you found one thing that you were going to change (the downward force you were going to apply to the ball) and another thing you thought might change as a result of changing the first thing (the height of the bounce).

Scientists call the thing we change on purpose the **independent variable**. We cause the change in the independent variable...so it changes **INDEPENDENTLY** of anything else in the experiment.

As a result of changing the independent variable, other variables in the experiment will change or respond. These are called the **dependent variables**. The value of the dependent variables **DEPENDS** on how you changed the independent variable. If you have difficulty remembering which is which, try thinking about it this way: the dependent variable is always the variable you are going to measure. Look at it in terms of our bouncing ball experiment: changing the independent variable (the increasing downward force of the ball) causes a change in the dependent variable (the bounce height of the ball) that you can measure.

Now let's develop a reasonable hypothesis by establishing a **cause and effect relationship**. We can use the word "if" for the cause part, and the word "then" for the effect part.

If I place increasing amounts of downward force on a ball, then the resulting bounce height will also increase.

Hypotheses do not always have to be expressed as *if/then* statements, but when you are starting out, *if/then* statements help make your hypotheses clear.

At this point, you were almost ready to carry out your scientific experiment, but you still had one detail left to think about:

How do I know the only possible cause of the ball bouncing higher is the increase in force I put on the ball?

There is only one way to be sure…and that is to make sure nothing else changes! The things you make sure you don't change are called **control variables**. A great way to remember this term is that you (the scientist performing the experiment) **CONTROL** these variables, to make sure they don't change. In your experiment, you could establish controls by making sure you used the same ball, threw it at the same surface and that no gusting winds or any other strange event affected your experiment.

So how did you design your experiment to test your hypothesis? Well, a reasonable start would be to throw your ball five or six times at the ground, making sure each time was harder than the last, and making mental notes (collecting data) to see if the ball bounced higher each time. You probably did exactly this — several times! — and were pretty pleased with yourself because you came to the **conclusion** that your hypothesis was supported by your data: the ball did go higher each time you threw it harder at the ground!

IMPORTANT NOTE!

Even if your hypothesis was not supported by your experiment, you would still gain VALUABLE knowledge. Experiments are NOT failures if they don't support their hypotheses, because you learn just as much from them!

Look at what you've done so far in scientific terms. You:

- developed a **question.**
- **researched** the question and looked at available data.
- developed a **hypothesis.**
- designed an experiment with appropriate **variables.**
- collected **data** from the experiment.
- drew a **conclusion** from the data.

Congratulations! Even at that early age, you completed all the steps in the most common **scientific process**.

It's important to understand that not all scientific processes happen in this order. You may have data in search of a hypothesis, or a hypothesis that needs more research. The point is to be orderly and consistent when you sit down to solve a problem.

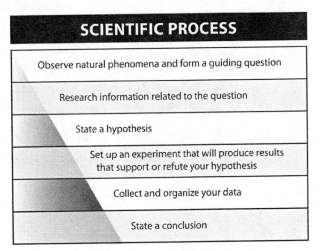

SCIENTIFIC PROCESS

Observe natural phenomena and form a guiding question

Research information related to the question

State a hypothesis

Set up an experiment that will produce results that support or refute your hypothesis

Collect and organize your data

State a conclusion

Figure 2.3 A Scientific Process

DEVELOPING A PROCEDURE

How would you update the bouncing ball investigation if you were to do it today? How would you make your variables more specific? What measurements would you need to make? What would the procedures look like? It's important for you to understand that you can't assume that the person reading your procedures will know anything about this experiment. So, you must be as clear and specific as possible. This is so your experiment can be repeated by yourself or others at a later date. Since you are much older now, let's make the guiding question a bit more advanced:

What is the relationship between the height from which a ball is dropped and the height to which it bounces?

Intuitively, you may already think that by increasing the height from which the ball is dropped, the ball will have more time to gain speed and will hit the ground with more force. So, let's update your hypothesis to reflect that.

If the height from which a ball is dropped is increased, then the resulting height of the first bounce will also increase.

Here are the updated variables to include in the investigation:

Independent Variable (the variable that you change) – height from which the ball is dropped

Dependent Variable (the responding variable that you measure) – height of the first bounce of the ball, after hitting the ground

Control Variables (things that you make sure are the same) – same ball, same bouncing surface, same measuring tools, same day and weather conditions

Now you are ready to design your experiment. You will organize it into a procedure consisting of **chronological** (ordered by time) steps. And then you will — hey, wait a minute!

This is your investigation! So, before we show you how WE would write the procedures for the experiment, why not try it for yourself? Remember, you'll need to decide what materials are necessary and state specific "step by step" instructions. What are you waiting for? Go write this down!

Once you have finished writing your own set of procedures, you may read on and see what we've come up with. It's possible that yours will be even better than ours.

Ball Bouncing Laboratory

Materials:

- one ball that you can fit into one hand — tennis ball, Super Ball™, etc.
- two meter sticks
- brick or cinderblock wall (that you can make chalk marks on)
- chalk

Procedure:

1. Find a place at school or home where you can make chalk marks on solid brick or cinder block walls. The ground the ball will bounce on should be as hard as possible — cement or asphalt are great surfaces to use.

2. Find a partner to work with. One of you will be dropping the ball and one of you will be marking how high it bounces. Decide who will measure and record the bounce height.

3. Tape the two meter sticks to the wall, one on top of the other, so that the first (lowest one) is touching the floor and the bottom of the second one touches the top of the first.

4. One student drops the ball from one meter off the ground. The other student makes a chalk dot on the wall next to the meter stick marking the height of the first bounce. Use the same point on the ball (top) when judging the height of the drop and the height of the bounce.

5. Record the height from which the ball is dropped and the height of the bounce.

6. Drop the ball at least two more times from each height.

7. Take the average of the bounce heights (height of first bounce + height of second bounce + height of third bounce all divided by three) and use it as the final measurement for that (bounce) height.

8. Increase the distance from which you drop the ball by ten centimeters and repeat steps 5, 6 and 7. Do this ten times — that means your last drop is from a height of 2 meters.

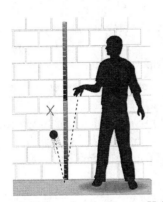

How similar was your procedure to ours? Is there anything you think we could do to improve ours? Is there anything you think you could do to improve yours? One critical component of the experiment is found in step 6, where the measurement is repeated. If your data is similar each time you repeat the measurement, it is more likely that your method is reliable. Another way to say this is that your experiment is **reproducible**. So, make sure to include repeat measurements in your experimental design.

Figure 2.4 Measuring the Bounce Height

CHAPTER 2 REVIEW

1. A judgement based on data gathered in an experiment is
   A. a skill.
   B. a conclusion.
   C. a hypothesis.
   D. an observation.

2. Andrika has learned that the hot water in her house is always gone by 6:30 a.m. She knows that this is because her sisters and mother always get to the shower before her. She decides to experiment with her morning routine to see if she can get a hot shower in the morning. Over the course of a week, she changes the time that she gets up, making it 10 minutes earlier each day. What is the dependent variable in this experiment?
   A. the time she gets up
   B. the volume of hot water her family uses
   C. the temperature of the water in the water heater
   D. the temperature of the water in Andrika's shower

3. A hypothesis is checked by
   A. research in journals.
   B. drawing a conclusion.
   C. experimentation.
   D. researching on the Internet.

4. Ryan wonders why his cola loses its carbonation as it warms. He knows that it is carbon dioxide that causes cola to fizz. Ryan decides to do a scientific experiment to research this phenomenon. What is the next step Ryan should take?
   A. ask a question
   B. draw a conclusion
   C. make an observation
   D. form a hypothesis

5. Thomas feels sleepy every day in science class. Science class is after lunch. He decides that he wants to be more alert and pay better attention to what his teacher is saying. He develops a hypothesis: if I eat healthier food at lunch, then I will have more energy to concentrate. Which experimental plan will **best** support or disprove his hypothesis?
   A. Design an experiment where he eats no lunch for a week, and then records how sleepy he felt each day.
   B. Design an experiment where he eats a chicken sandwich and fruit for lunch for a week, and then records how sleepy he felt each day.
   C. Design an experiment where he records what he ate for breakfast each day, and then records how sleepy he felt later in class.
   D. Design an experiment where he sleeps through lunch each day, and then records if he is hungry in class afterward.

1. Ⓐ Ⓑ Ⓒ Ⓓ
2. Ⓐ Ⓑ Ⓒ Ⓓ
3. Ⓐ Ⓑ Ⓒ Ⓓ
4. Ⓐ Ⓑ Ⓒ Ⓓ
5. Ⓐ Ⓑ Ⓒ Ⓓ

Chapter 3
Equipment and Measurement

SCIENTIFIC MEASUREMENT

Scientists often make measurements to quantify a certain phenomenon observed in the world around them.

Let's say that Tariq's teacher has asked him to measure the length of the classroom. How would he do it? There are a few important points to remember:

- All measurements must have a unit. If Tariq measures the length of his classroom and announces that it is 16.7, it doesn't mean much. Yards, meters, feet? We need a unit.
- All units must be common. What if Tariq tells us that the room is 16.7 lengths of *his* feet? Great. Now we have to measure Tariq's feet in order to derive the length of the room.
- All units must be common *everywhere*. Tariq finally gets it together and tells us that the room measures 16.7 standard feet. Well, now *we* know the length of the room, but no one in Japan or Germany will understand the measurement, because the rest of the world uses the metric system.

The United States has been a bit slow to comply, but metric units are now increasingly used in this country. Let's look at the units and equipment appropriate to a few common measurements in the lab.

THE RIGHT TOOLS FOR THE RIGHT JOBS

No matter how good your procedure is, it is not worth much if you cannot collect any data from it. The measurements that you make are your data. In order to make the measurements, you need the right tools. If you are in doubt about this, consider the following scenarios.

- trying to paint your nails with a paint roller
- washing the car with a Brillo® pad
- using a can of soup to hammer in a nail

These are silly examples, but that is only because you know exactly what tool to use to paint you nails, wash the car or hammer in a nail. You are learning the process of science now, and some tools will be unfamiliar to you at first. So, we will start with three basic tools: the meter stick, the balance and the graduated cylinder.

LENGTH

In this investigation, you used a **meter stick** to measure the height from which the ball was dropped and how high it bounced. A meter stick is the perfect tool for measuring linear (straight-line) distances. Meter sticks measure distance in basic metric units called **meters**. Sometimes you need a smaller tool than the meter stick. Then you may use a ruler. Rulers are usually marked in fractions of meters, called centimeters, and also in inches.

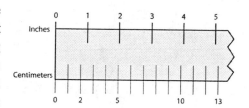

Figure 3.1 Meter Stick

Centimeters and inches are different kinds of units. A centimeter is 1/10 of a meter; an inch is 1/12 of a foot. Meters are a unit defined by the **International System** (SI) to measure the distance dimensions (length, width and height) of an object. One meter equals about three **U.S. Customary System** feet. SI units are used by scientists all over the world, instead of regional units like the U.S. Customary system. This makes it easier for scientists to compare data without converting the units.

MASS

Now let's change our thinking a bit and consider how you could expand the bouncing ball investigation. Let's say you wanted to compare bounces of similarly sized balls that had different **masses.** When you modify the experiment, you might also need to change the tools you use. To measure mass, you use a balance.

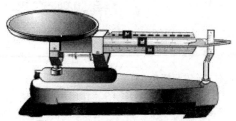

Figure 3.2 Triple-Beam Balance

Balances measure mass in units called **grams**. They are different than grocery store scales, which measure in ounces and pounds (U.S. Customary System units). Figure 3.2 shows a triple-beam balance, which is a great tool. Even more accurate, however, is the analytical balance, which has a digital display that tells you the mass to 4 decimal places.

VOLUME

Now let's say we wanted to compare how much space is taken up by several types of balls. Here, we are comparing their **volumes.** We use a tool called a **graduated cylinder** to measure volume. Liquid volume is measured in SI units called **liters**.

The best way to measure volume using a graduated cylinder is to get at eye level with the numbers printed on its side.

Figure 3.3 Graduated Cylinder

Don't look at the cylinder from a position above or below the cylinder, because the volume will appear different than it actually is. Looking directly at the cylinder, as in Figure 3.3, will allow you to read the volume of the liquid properly. Sometimes the surface of the liquid will appear curved. This is called the **meniscus.** If the meniscus is curved upward like a smile, the volume is read from the lowest part of the curve. This is the case with water and most other liquids, and is shown in Figure 3.3. If the meniscus curves downward like a frown, the volume is read from the top of the curve.

So, the meter, gram and liter are the three base units of the SI system. Table 3.1 compares these units with their US Customary System counterparts.

Table 3.1 English-Metric Conversions

English		Metric
Length		
1 inches (in)	=	2.54 cm
3.281 ft	=	1 m
Mass		
0.035 oz	=	1 g
1 lb	=	0.453 kg
Volume		
33.8 fl oz	=	1 L
1 gal	=	3.78 L

Another common laboratory measurement is temperature. **Temperature** measures how hot or cold something is. All measurements for temperature are taken in degrees. In the metric system, **Celsius** is the unit of temperature. The SI unit for temperature is **Kelvin**, and the English unit is **Fahrenheit**. Both Celsius and Fahrenheit are written in their abbreviated forms with a degree symbol, as in °C and °F, whereas Kelvin is abbreviated simply as K (not degrees Kelvin). To convert from one unit to another, use the following formulas:

$$C = \frac{(F - 32)}{1.8} \qquad F = 1.8\,C + 32 \qquad C = K - 273.15 \qquad K = C + 273.15$$

C is degrees Celsius; **F** is degrees Fahrenheit; **K** is Kelvin.

Figure 3.4 Temperature Conversion Formulas

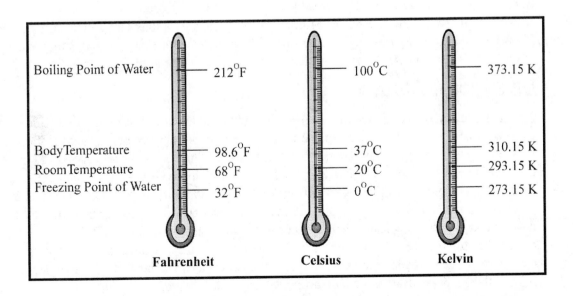

CHANGING THE MAGNITUDE

The SI system is also called the **metric system**. This term is probably familiar to you. Metric system units are defined in multiples of 10 from the **base unit**. The metric prefixes indicate which multiple of 10 — 10, 100 or 1,000 — the base unit should be multiplied or divided by. The table below is set up to help you know how far and in which direction to move a decimal point when making conversions from one unit to another.

Table 3.2 Changing the Magnitude of a Unit

Prefix	kilo (k)	hecto (h)	deka (da)	Base Unit	deci (d)	centi (c)	milli (m)
Abbreviation	km	hm	dam	**meter**	dm	cm	mm
	kL	hL	daL	**Liter**	dL	cL	mL
	kg	hg	dag	**gram**	dg	cg	mg
Multiplication Factor (from the base unit)	1000	100	10	**1**	0.1	0.01	0.001

Multiply when changing from a larger unit to a smaller one. Divide when changing from a smaller unit to a larger one. (Remember, dividing is the same as multiplying by a fraction.) Let's look at two examples.

Let's say you have a bowling ball with a mass of 4.54 kilograms (kg). To convert kg to grams (g), move three spaces to the right on the table. Each of those spaces represents a multiplication factor of 10. Since $10 \times 10 \times 10 = 1000$, you multiply by 1000.

$$\textbf{4.54 kg} \times 1000 = \textbf{4,540 kg}$$

Here's another example. A soda can has a volume of 355 milliliters (mL). To convert mL to deciliters (dL), you move two spaces to the left. Since $10 \times 10 = 100$, you divide by 100, which is the same as multiplying by 0.01.

$$\textbf{355 mL} \div 100 = \textbf{355 mL} \times 0.01 = \textbf{3.55 dL}$$

Some abbreviations, like the deciliter (dL), may be unfamiliar to you. In the science lab, and in most real-life applications, kilo-, centi- and milli- will be the abbreviations that you most often encounter. However, all these units are correct, and some of the lesser-known ones are even common in particular industries. The hectometer (hm), for instance, is a commonly used unit in agriculture and forestry.

DIMENSIONAL ANALYSIS

Now that we have covered the units themselves and talked about adjusting their magnitude, we need to discuss converting the identity of the units. This is important because you will often encounter measurements in common units (remember Tariq's feet?) which must be converted to SI units. This is done by the process of dimensional analysis. **Dimensional analysis** is a structured method of helping you to convert units by using conversion factors. A dimension is a property that can be measured, such as length, time, mass or temperature. It may also be derived by multiplying or dividing other dimensions. Some examples of derived dimensions include length/time (velocity), length^3 (volume) or mass/length^3 (density). Dimensions are *not* the same as units. The dimensions of a physical quantity can be measured in any appropriate unit. For instance, velocity can be measured in mph, m/s, etc., but it will always be a measure of length divided by time. Therefore, the dimensions of velocity are length/time.

A **conversion factor** is a defined relationship between two units. They are similar to the expressions shown in Table 3.2, but they are written as fractions that are always equal to 1. For instance, the conversion from inches to centimeters is 1 in = 2.54 cm. We can write two conversion factors using this information:

$$\frac{1 \text{ in}}{2.54 \text{ cm}} \quad \textbf{and} \quad \frac{2.54 \text{ cm}}{1 \text{ in}}$$

To convert given quantities in one set of units to their equivalent values in another set of units, we set up dimensional equations. We will write our dimensional equations so that the old units cancel and we are left with only the new units. So you will have to choose which form of the conversion factor you need to use. How will you know? In order to eliminate a unit in the numerator, you will need to cancel it out by choosing a conversion factor that places that unit in the denominator. Likewise, if you want to eliminate a unit that is in the denominator, you will choose a conversion factor that places that unit in the numerator. Because any factor divided by itself is equal to 1, this process will eliminate factors that you do not need.

Example: How many centimeters are in 4 feet?

Step 1. Begin by writing the term that needs to be converted:

$$4 \text{ ft}$$

Step 2. Identify the unit that the term needs to be converted into:

$$4 \text{ ft} = \underline{} \text{ cm}$$

Step 3. Next, identify the conversion formulas that will be needed:

$$12 \text{ in} = 1 \text{ ft } \textbf{and } 1 \text{ in} = 2.54 \text{ cm}$$

Step 4. Write both forms of the conversion factors as fractions:

$$\frac{12 \text{in}}{1 \text{ft}} \text{ and } \frac{1 \text{ft}}{12 \text{in}} \quad + \quad \frac{1 \text{in}}{2.54 \text{cm}} \text{ and } \frac{2.54 \text{cm}}{1 \text{in}}$$

Step 5. Select the correct conversion factors that will eliminate unwanted units:

$$4 \text{ft} \times \frac{12 \text{in}}{1 \text{ft}} \times \frac{2.54 \text{cm}}{1 \text{in}} = \underline{} \text{ cm}$$

Step 6. Cross out the units that cancel and multiply the rest together:

$$4 \cancel{\text{ft}} \times \frac{12 \cancel{\text{in}}}{1 \cancel{\text{ft}}} \times \frac{2.54 \text{cm}}{1 \cancel{\text{in}}} \times = 121.92 \text{cm}$$

Notice that the units of "inches" and "feet" cancel, leaving you with centimeters.

WRONG: If you had used the conversion factors incorrectly, this is what you would have:

$$4 \text{ft} \times \frac{1 \text{ft}}{12 \text{in}} \times \frac{1 \text{in}}{2.54 \text{cm}} = \frac{4 \text{ft}^2 \cdot \text{in}}{30.4 \text{in} \cdot \text{cm}}$$

Notice, feet multiplied by feet are feet squared (ft^2). None of the units cancel, so you know right away that this is a wrong approach.

RATIO AND PROPORTIONALITY

Metric unit conversions are a good springboard for another concept: **ratio**. A ratio is a unitless quantity that compares one measurement relative to another. Ratios are often expressed as two numbers, separated by a colon, as in 2:3, which can be read as "two parts of one thing for every three parts of another." Let's be more specific. Here are some examples:

- A centimeter is $1/10^{th}$ of a meter. The ratio of centimeters to meters is 1:10.
- A water molecule (H_2O) contains two hydrogen atoms for every one oxygen atom. The ratio of hydrogen to oxygen is 2:1.
- A basket containing six brown puppies and two golden puppies represents a ratio of brown to gold puppies that can be described as 6:2 or 3:1.

When two changing quantities exhibit a constant ratio, they are said to be **proportional**. This can be stated mathematically as

$$y = k \times x$$

Here, y is the result of the change of the variable x. The term k is the **proportionality constant**. When constant, this equation is a line, and k is its slope. (If you've taken algebra, you might think of this as m.) Where does the ratio come in? Think of it another way:

$$k = \frac{y}{x}$$

Here, k defines the ratio of y to x. (Have you heard the phrase "rise over run"?)

Ratio and proportionality are commonly used in all fields of science. In physical science, you will use ratio and proportionality to determine the relationships between velocity and acceleration and between work and force.

PRECISION AND ACCURACY

What is the difference between precision and accuracy? Many people use these terms interchangeably, but they are not the same. **Accuracy** refers to how "correct" a measurement is. If Tariq measured his classroom's length as 16.7 feet (5.09 meters), but a blueprint of the building indicated that is was actually 16.1 feet, then his measurement was not accurate.

Precision refers to how small a scale is being used to make a measurement. The smaller the scale, the more precise the measurement. For example, a measurement made to the nearest eighth of an inch is more precise than a measurement that is rounded to the nearest inch. There is a practical limit to this concept. For example, if Tariq measured the room down to the nearest nanometer (0.000000001 meter), it really wouldn't have more practical meaning than measuring it to the nearest millimeter (0.001 meter), would it?

Practice Exercise:

Look at the two thermometers below. Which one would give you a more precise temperature reading?

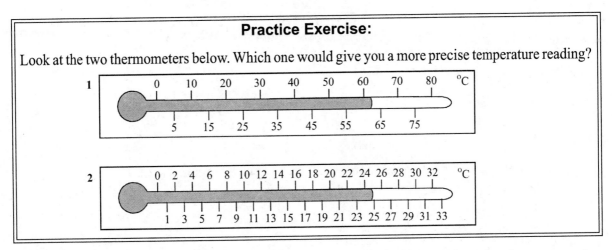

Defining precision in terms of the number of significant figures leads us to another important point about precision. The smaller the scale on which a measurement is made, the more distinct the measurements can be. Let's think of an example to illustrate this.

Three small water samples are collected by Adam and Trisha. Adam uses a 100 mL graduated cylinder; Trisha uses a 10 mL graduated cylinder. Their data is below.

Sample	Adam's Volume Measurement	Trisha's Volume Measurement
1	8 mL	8.27 mL
2	8 mL	8.54 mL
3	8 mL	8.31 mL

Adam cannot make a good assessment of the volume of his sample, because his instrument is not precise enough. Trisha can clearly see, with her more precise glassware, that she collected three water samples with distinctly different volumes.

It is important to note that measurements can be made very precisely, but not accurately. They can also be made accurately, but not precisely. A good way to compare the two is shown in Figure 3.6. The bull's eye in the center is the "accepted value" that you want to hit. The first instance shows random hits that are far from the center. So the precision and accuracy are both poor. The precision is good when the darts all hit the same location. The dart throws are accurate when they hit close to the bull's eye. But only when the darts hit close together and hit the center are the throws both precise <u>and</u> accurate.

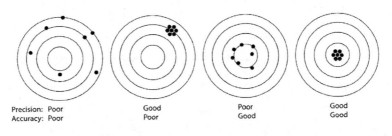

Figure 3.6 Precision and Accuracy

CHAPTER 3 REVIEW

1. Kilograms are a unit of measurement for

    A. mass.
    B. height.
    C. volume.
    D. size.

2. Identify the correct conversion of 4.2 grams (g) to kilograms (kg).

    A. 4.2 g = 0.0042 kg
    B. 4.2 g = 0.042 kg
    C. 4.2 g = 42 kg
    D. 4.2 g = 4,200 kg

3. Identify the reason why scientists from countries around the world use the same measurement system.

    A. to simplify international patent laws
    B. to make it easier to understand and compare published results
    C. to make it easier for scientists to misrepresent their results
    D. to simplify the laws of physics

4. Graduated cylinders are marked in units of

    A. grams.   B. meters.   C. millimeters.   D. milliliters.

5. Absolute zero is the theoretical temperature of minimum atomic or molecular motion. Absolute zero is reached at 0K. What is absolute 0 in units of Celsius?

    A. -273.15° C
    B. 0° C
    C. -134° C
    D. 134° C

| 1. Ⓐ Ⓑ Ⓒ Ⓓ |
| 2. Ⓐ Ⓑ Ⓒ Ⓓ |
| 3. Ⓐ Ⓑ Ⓒ Ⓓ |
| 4. Ⓐ Ⓑ Ⓒ Ⓓ |
| 5. Ⓐ Ⓑ Ⓒ Ⓓ |

Chapter 4
Data and Its Presentation

OBSERVATION AND DESCRIPTION

Let's go back to the beginning and define the purpose of **scientific investigation**. In a very general sense, scientific investigation helps us learn *what* things are, and *how* or *why* they work the way they do. In order to launch a scientific investigation, you will need to make some observations. As you will recall from Chapter 2, an **observation** is anything that you notice with one of your five senses. Sometimes your senses must be enhanced (that is, made more sensitive) in order to see or hear something. Therefore, observations can also be made with the help of technology, including instruments like microscopes or telescopes.

There are two kinds of observations — **Qualitative** and **Quantitative**.

Qualitative observations **describe** objects or events using language and/or drawings. To put it another way, qualitative observations are really descriptions of what you experienced. These descriptions can answer the question "what is it?" with specific details.

Another way to convey qualitative information is with a diagram. A **diagram** is a drawing, sketch or outline designed to demonstrate or explain an observation. A diagram can also be used to illustrate a process, like the procedure of an experiment. You have already seen several diagrams in this text. In fact, look back at Figure 2.4. That diagram gave you a visual representation (that is, a picture) of what the experimental procedure described in words. Look also at the right side of Figure 4.1, where the instructor is drawing a diagram of the movement of electrons during the course of a chemical reaction.

Figure 4.1 Qualitative Observations

Some qualitative observations are **subjective**. This means that they depend on the person observing. One example is color. Three different people could view the same object and describe its color differently.

Quantitative observations, on the other hand, involve numbers and measurements. Quantitative observations are more **objective** than qualitative descriptions, meaning that they depend less on who observes them. That is important to a scientist, so scientists tend to set up experiments that generate quantitative measurements — that is, **data**. In the bouncing ball experiment from Chapter 2, the recorded bounce height was quantitative data.

Figure 4.2 Quantitative Observations

RECORDING AND PRESENTING THE DATA

Let's look again at the bouncing ball investigation. Our procedure indicated that you should mark the height of the bounce on the wall. Then, of course, you measure the bounce heights. But now you need to make an important choice: how should you record (and display) your data?

A great way to record and present the data from an investigation is to use a **data table**. Data tables present data in columns and rows and make it easier to compare things side-by-side.

Here is a table showing a set of results for the bouncing ball investigation:

Table 4.1 Bouncing Ball Sample Data

Height from which ball is dropped (meters)	Trial 1 Height of first bounce (meters)	Trial 2 Height of first bounce (meters)	Trial 3 Height of first bounce (meters)	Average of 3 Trials Trial 1 + Trial 2 +Trial 3 / 3
1.0	0.5	0.6	0.5	0.53
1.1	0.6	0.7	0.6	0.63
1.2	0.7	0.7	0.8	0.73
1.3	0.8	0.8	0.8	0.80
1.4	0.8	0.9	0.9	0.87
1.5	1.0	1.0	1.0	1.00
1.6	1.1	1.2	1.1	1.13
1.7	1.2	1.2	1.3	1.23
1.8	1.3	1.3	1.3	1.30
1.9	1.5	1.4	1.5	1.47
2.0	1.6	1.5	1.5	1.53

Data tables aren't the only way to record and present data. Other ways of presenting data are **graphs** and **charts**. We use these ways of presenting data because they make the data easier to understand and interpret.

Line graphs are helpful in pointing out **trends**. Notice that in Figure 4.3, you can use a ruler to draw a line extending beyond the data you collected. This is called **extrapolation**. It allows you to make a **prediction**. Examine Figure 4.3: if the drop height were increased to 2.5m, we would expect to see a bounce height of just over 2m. Get out your ruler and see for yourself.

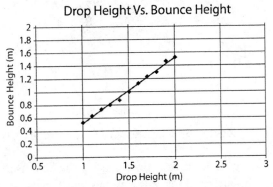

Figure 4.3 Line Graph Showing Increasing Bounce Height, with Increased Drop

A line graph lets you identify trends because it shows a direct relationship between your independent variable and your dependent (responding) variable. (Remember cause and effect, from Chapter 2?) In this case, the line graph shows the relationship between the height from which the ball is dropped, and the height of the first bounce. When plotting line graphs, the **independent variable** is plotted on the **x-axis** (horizontal axis), and the **dependent variable** is plotted on the **y-axis** (vertical axis).

Sometimes line graphs are also used to compare multiple sets of data (experimental results). For example, you'd want to use a multiple line graph if you did the same experiment using three different kinds of balls.

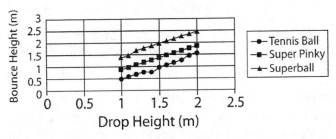

Figure 4.4 Multiple Line Graph Comparing Three Different Balls

Bar graphs are some of the easiest data presentations to read. The bar graph below shows the average bounces of the three different kinds of balls dropped from 2 meters.

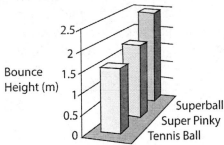

Figure 4.5 Bar Graph Comparing Bounce Height of Three Balls at the 2-Meter Drop Height

Circle graphs (or pie charts) are useful for showing parts of whole. For instance, let's say that 16% of our trials were done with a tennis ball, 64% with a Super Pinky and 20% with a Super Ball. Notice the percentage of different balls used. Since this adds up to 100%, you can put this data in a circle graph.

Superball   Tennis Ball

Super Pinky

Figure 4.6 Circle Graph Showing Types of Balls Used

What data presentation all boils down to is this: making the data useful to both the investigator and his audience. Presenting data in different formats gives us a different perspective and helps us interpret the meaning of the data.

MATHEMATICAL TOOLS IN PRESENTATIONS

Graphs are not the only way to interpret data. Sometimes scientists look for trends in the data by examining the **range** of answers. The range is the difference between the smallest and largest value. The range tells you how "spread out" the data is. Data with large ranges are more spread out. In our ball experiment, the average bounce height of a ball dropped from 1 meter is 0.53 meters (Table 4.1). The range of the individual bounces is:

$$0.6 \text{ meters} - 0.5 \text{ meters} = 0.1 \text{ meters}$$

Other times, scientists want to find out the mathematical "center" of the data. These kinds of interpretations of data are part of a much larger field of mathematics called **statistics**. Three statistical tools that are extremely useful in science to find the "center" of data are the **mean** and **median**.

The **mean** in a set of data is the sum of a list of numbers, divided by the total number of numbers in the list. This may sound familiar to you because it is similar to a term you already understand (and probably have used before) called the **average**. On our data table (Table 4.1) we labeled the last column "Average of 3 Trials," but we just as easily could have called it the **mean** of the three trials.

The **median** in a set of data is the exact "middle value" of a list. To find the median, you have to put the values in order from lowest to highest and then find the number that is exactly in the middle. If the list has an odd number of entries, the median is the middle entry in the sorted list. If the list has an even number of entries, the median is equal to the sum of the two middle numbers divided by two. In our ball experiment, here's how we'd find the median of the average (mean) bounces:

0.53 meters	1
0.63 meters	2
0.73 meters	3
0.8 meters	4
0.87 meters	5
1 meter	**6**
1.13 meters	7
1.23 meters	8
1.3 meters	9
1.47 meters	10
1.53 meters	11

(1) List the data in order.

(2) The **median** is the middle entry — in this case, entry #6 — which has a value of 1 meter

Sometimes it is important to know what the most common experimental measurement is. The **mode** in a set of data is the most common (frequent) value. There can be more than one mode in a set of data if there is a "tie" for how frequently numbers are used. It is also possible that there is no mode at all in a set of data if all the numbers are used the same number of times...and this is true for our ball experiment. For practice, though, let's say we had a data set like this:

50 55 60 60 60 75 80 85 90

The mode of this set of data is 60, because it appears three times on the list (and all the other numbers only appear once).

INFERENCE AND EXPLANATION

When a scientist wants to take an investigation to a deeper level than either qualitative or quantitative observations, he or she **explains** and **infers**.

When scientists **explain** the outcome of an investigation, they are trying to tell the world why the experiment produced the result that it did. The scientists involved are using their own prior experiences in forming the explanation. So, by their very nature, explanations are **subjective** (remember, that's the opposite of objective). Good explanations must be supported by a lot of data and evidence, and statistics are often used. However, even a good explanation may not accurately reflect reality.

Scientists frequently move even further into the subjective, by making **inferences**. Inferring is a reasoning process. A scientist applies what he or she already knows to new data and interprets it in such a way as to "make it make sense." Figure 4.3 and 4.4 show a pretty consistent upward trend in the bounce height, with increasing drop height. As a scientist, you could make the inference that bounce height would continue to increase with increasing drop height.

But beware: inferences are not always logical, and there is always a practical limit to a trend. For instance, if you dropped your Super Pinky from a commercial airliner at an altitude of 10,000 meters, it's more likely that it would completely break apart when it hits the ground, rather than bounce as high as the trend predicted by Figure 4.4 might suggest.

Although both explanations and inferences can be incorrect, they are INDISPENSABLE! You have to make explanations and inferences in order to generate a conclusion. As you know, a **conclusion** is a summary statement that takes into account all of your observations, explanations and inferences. It shows what you learned from your experiment.

Sometimes, though, a conclusion shows *what you still don't know.* You may find that your conclusion is unsatisfactory or feel that it needs more testing. In that case, you will need to generate a new hypothesis and start all over again!

Challenge Activity

Examine the cartoons below. Make an observation and at least one inference about each one. One example is done for you.

1.

Observation: There are three baby birds in the nest.
Inference: The baby birds in the nest are hungry.

2.

3.

4.

5.

6.

OBTAINING UNEXPECTED RESULTS

Unexpected results can occur during a scientific investigation. They can be a result of error, such as improper equipment usage, improper setup or poor data collection. However, when these factors are carefully controlled, unexpected results can lead to better and more complete hypotheses.

ANALYSIS OF ERROR IN SCIENTIFIC DATA

Any errors made during an experiment will result in a distortion of data. The following are examples of errors that can be made during an experiment.

- A student consistently reads the volume in a graduated cylinder at a slight angle instead of straight on. The recorded volume will be consistently high or low.

- Sometimes a spillage or other accident can result in an invalid data point.

- Pouring a liquid from one container to another and then recording the volume will usually result in some error since not all of the liquid will be transferred to the second container.

- Uncalibrated instruments have a zero measurement that is not zero. That is, an empty, uncalibrated balance may still read 2 grams even though there is nothing in the pan. Calibrate your instruments in order to get good results.

- Errors in data are commonly made simply by recording the data incorrectly.

Compare the data obtained by two students performing the same experiment. What is the relationship between the length of time and the degrees of temperature change? Student 1 might suggest that for every five minutes of time that elapsed, the temperature dropped five degrees. Student 2 has recorded data that suggests otherwise — the relationship between the length of time and the degrees of temperature change is quite different in his results. What can you infer?

Table 4.2 Time for Water to Freeze – Student 1

Data from Student 1	0	5	10	15	20	25	35
Temperature of salt water	25°C	20°C	15°C	10° C	5°C	0°C	-10°C

Table 4.3 Time for Water to Freeze – Student 2

Data from Student 2	0	5	10	15	20	25	35
Temperature of salt water	25°C	20°C	25°C	10°C	−5°C	0°C	−10°C

A careful analysis of the data would indicate that water does not suddenly warm 5 degrees or drop 15 degrees in temperature when placed in a freezer. An error must have been made either in the experiment or in recording the data. By repeating the experiment and carefully checking the data for any variations in the control, an analysis of the error can be made.

CHAPTER 4 REVIEW

1. Large amounts of petrified wood are found in northeast Arizona. Using inductive reasoning, four inferences are made. Which is the **most** reasonable?

    A.   All wood becomes petrified.

    B.   No forests grew in other parts of Arizona.

    C.   A forest once stood there.

    D.   Wood only becomes petrified in northeast Arizona.

2. Which of the following phrases contains quantitative data?

    A. Green leaves surround white flowers.

    B. Ricky's football jersey is number 85.

    C. Seeds sprout more quickly when it is warm.

    D. Water evaporated at a rate of 2 mL per minute.

Stacy made a volume measurement 9 times. Her data is below.

    10.2   10.1   10.1   10.3   10.2   10.3   10.1   10.1   10.2

3. What is the mode of Stacey's data set?

    A.   10.2

    B.   10.1

    C.   0.2

    D.   10.17

4. What is the range of Stacey's data set?

    A.   10.2

    B.   10.1

    C.   0.2

    D.   10.17

5. What is the mean of Stacey's data set?

    A.   10.2

    B.   10.1

    C.   0.2

    D.   10.17

1. Ⓐ Ⓑ Ⓒ Ⓓ
2. Ⓐ Ⓑ Ⓒ Ⓓ
3. Ⓐ Ⓑ Ⓒ Ⓓ
4. Ⓐ Ⓑ Ⓒ Ⓓ
5. Ⓐ Ⓑ Ⓒ Ⓓ

Chapter 5
Laboratory Safety

Walking into science class on Monday morning, you see that materials are all set up for a lab. YES! You love lab days because you get to actually DO science. You observe the classroom on the way to your seat. Before doing anything else, you draw a picture of what you see going on in the classroom. The picture looks something like the one below.

Figure 5.1 A Classroom in Chaos

Your teacher sees your drawing and is horrified! Clearly, many students have forgotten the lab safety rules that were reviewed on Friday. She asks your permission to photocopy it for the class. Then she passes it out for homework the next day as a part of the following assignment:

1. What are two unsafe activities shown in the illustration? Why are they unsafe?

2. List two correct lab procedures depicted in the illustration.

3. What should Bob do after the accident?

4. What should Sue do to avoid an accident?

5. Find three things shown in the lab that should not be there.

6. Compare Joe's and Carl's lab techniques. Who is doing it the correct way?

7. List three items in the illustration that are there for the safety of the students in the lab.

Before reading on, please take some time to examine the picture and answer the questions for yourself. Then we'll give you our perspective.

1. What are two unsafe activities shown in the illustration? Why are they unsafe?

There is SO much to choose from! Let's take the activities of Tim and Ray first. Tim is hitting Ray over the head with a book. This is a DEFINITE no-no. First, Ray could get hurt. Additionally, other people could get hurt, even if they are not fooling around. *No horseplay is allowed in the lab; accidents happen when people are not paying attention.*

Next, take a look at what Joe and Jim are about to do: they are about to drink their experiment. That is EXTREMELY unsafe. *When in the laboratory, you should never put anything to your nose or mouth, unless specifically directed by your teacher to do so.*

2. List two correct lab procedures depicted in the illustration.

Tina is doing a great job holding the test tube over the flame with the proper tool (called tongs). She also has the test tube pointing away from herself and others. Carl and Tina are both wearing proper safety goggles and are focused on their work.

3. What should Bob do after the accident?

The first thing Bob should do is *let the teacher know the accident has occurred!* In fact, that is what all students should do ANY time there is an accident in the lab. Next he should (carefully) clean up the glass with a glass collection broom and dustpan. He should make sure to *follow his teacher's directions* on whether to put the broken glass in the trash can or into another receptacle that might be designated specifically for glass.

4. What should Sue do to avoid an accident?

Never leave long hair loose in the lab. Sue may not like this, but if she doesn't do something to pin down her beautiful golden locks of hair they are going to catch on fire! Given the choice between securing her hair and having it singed, she'll choose to find a hair clip or hair band!

5. What are three things shown in the lab that should not be there?

Some of these are obvious, and some are not. Well, first, there is a rabbit loose in class! If you look closely, you'll see a pair of scissors that definitely should not be in the electric socket. Third, there should not be a beaker and spill on the floor next to Tim. Now you name three more unsafe situations.

_____

_____

_____

_____

_____

6. Compare Joe's and Carl's lab techniques. Who is doing it the correct way?

Way to go Carl! Just say NO to Joe! *Never put anything in the lab in your mouth, especially not a liquid that is labeled with the symbol for poison!*

7. List three items in the illustration that are there for the safety of the students in the lab.

If you look in the upper right hand corner you should see the *fire extinguisher, safety blanket and first aid box*. It's important to know where all three of these items are located at all times. They are there for your safety and the safety of others. Of course, in our picture, the first aid kit is flapping open and the fire extinguisher is missing. *Let your teacher know if laboratory safety equipment is damaged or missing.*

It's also important to note that some of the students are *wearing safety glasses*. You should know where these are and make sure to wear them during lab.

The most important safety precautions you can take in a science lab are to *always follow instructions*, and when something happens that shouldn't make sure to *inform your teacher as soon as possible*.

Scavenger Hunt!
Find one picture in Chapters 1 – 4 of this book that shows a student behaving unsafe.
Did you find it? Eureka!
What should the student do to "fix" the unsafe behavior?

THINK WHILE YOU WORK

The ability to **infer causes** and **predict outcomes** should not only be applied to your experiments. You must apply these skills in life also! They will help you make reasonable decisions about many things, including safe behavior in the lab. The following activities will show you how.

Challenge Activity

Rodrigo fills a glass beaker with distilled water and places it on a hotplate. He heats the water, measuring the temperature every three minutes. His results are shown below.

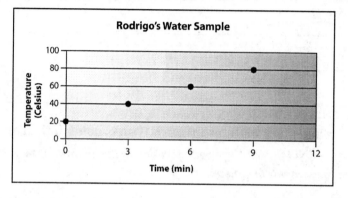

1. What temperature did the water sample start at? Was it warm or cold?

2. What do you predict the temperature will be at 12 minutes?

3. When the experiment is over, should Rodrigo remove the beaker from the hot plate with his bare hands?

4. Is it safe to breathe around the boiling sample, or should Rodrigo wear a face mask?

Challenge Activity

Marita places a beaker containing chemical A on a triple beam balance. She records the mass. She adds chemical B to the beaker and records the mass. As the chemicals begin to react, fumes are produced, and mass is lost. Marita reads the mass of the beaker every 10 seconds and records the mass lost. Her results are shown below.

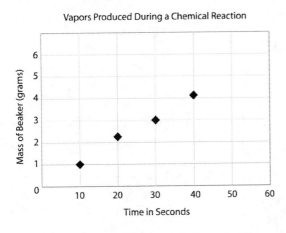

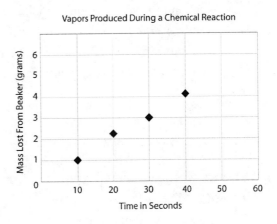

1. Which of the graphs above correctly illustrates Marita's laboratory experiment?
2. Where should this experiment be performed?
3. Predict how many grams will be lost at the 60-second mark.
4. Where has the mass gone?

Challenge Activity

Circle graphs (or pie charts) are another way of presenting data. They show parts of a whole. For instance, let's look at the data from an imaginary study. The study shows the percentage of all laboratory injuries that are caused by certain unsafe activities. Each activity is a slice of the pie. The results are shown below.

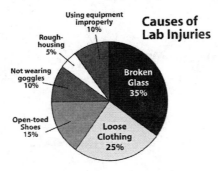

1. Based on this graph, what can you infer to be the greatest threat to student safety?
2. Look back at Figure 5.1. Which students in the figure are practicing the unsafe behaviors shown in this circle graph?
3. Make a circle graph of your own, based on Figure 5.1. How many students are practicing each unsafe behavior?
4. Does your circle graph show the same patterns as the national study? Why do you think there are differences?

CHAPTER 5 REVIEW

1. Various safety rules apply in the laboratory. In order to protect your clothing, you should
   A. wear an laboratory smock or lab coat.
   B. wear clothing treated with Teflon.
   C. wear clothing treated with Scotchgard™.
   D. wear as many layers as possible.

2. Reaching across a flame is
   A. never acceptable.
   B. always acceptable.
   C. sometimes acceptable.
   D. seldom acceptable.

3. Identify when you should report a chemical spill to your teacher.
   A. immediately
   B. after you've cleaned up the spill
   C. only if you think the spill is dangerous
   D. after you've finished the experiment so your results are not ruined

4. Identify the lab activity that should be conducted under a fume hood.
   A. measuring very high velocities
   B. using high voltage sources of laser light
   C. mixing chemicals that produce dangerous vapors
   D. massing a series of objects

5. What is the best way to avoid eye damage from chemical splashes in the laboratory?
   A. Wear your eyeglasses.
   B. Wear your contact lenses.
   C. Wear your safety glasses or goggles over your eyeglasses or contact lenses.
   D. Stay near the eyewash station and first aid kit throughout class.

1. Ⓐ Ⓑ Ⓒ Ⓓ
2. Ⓐ Ⓑ Ⓒ Ⓓ
3. Ⓐ Ⓑ Ⓒ Ⓓ
4. Ⓐ Ⓑ Ⓒ Ⓓ
5. Ⓐ Ⓑ Ⓒ Ⓓ

Unit 1 Review
Characteristic of Science

Paolo performed Internet research to discover the average height of 6 different types of clouds. His data is below. Use it to answer questions 1 and 2.

Cloud Type	Altitude (m)
Stratus	1800
Cumulonimbus	2500
Altostratus	4800
Altocumulus	6000
Cirrostratus	6100
Cirrus	7200

1. Which of the following graphs depicts Paolo's data most clearly?

A.

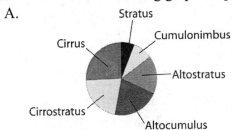

C.

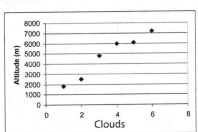

B.

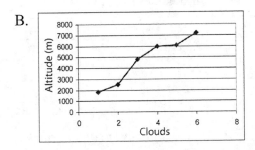

D.

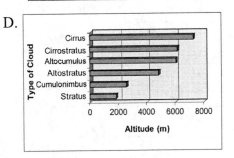

2. Select a correct inference from the following statements.

   A. No clouds form beneath 1800 meters.

   B. No stratus clouds can be found at 2000 meters.

   C. All cirrus clouds are found at 7200 meters.

   D. Altocumulus clouds form at air pressures similar to cirrostratus clouds.

The class hamsters Ron and Lucy had a litter of baby hamsters. One was white, two were brown, three were brown and white striped and two were black. When the baby hamsters are ready to eat adult hamster food, the class debates which brand is best to feed them. Tom votes for Brand A, because the box says that it will give the hamsters a glossy coat. Lawson votes for Brand B because the box claims that it will give the hamsters strong teeth. Tawanna votes for Brand C because the box claims that veterinarians most often recommend that brand for overall hamster health. The class decides to divide the hamsters into groups and compare their progress. Use this information to answer questions 3 – 5.

3. Which table defines the experimental groups that will allow the students to choose among the brands?

A.

1 white hamster	2 brown hamsters	3 brown & white hamsters	2 black hamsters
Brand A	Brand B	Brand C	Mother's milk

B.

1 white hamster	2 brown hamsters	3 brown & white hamsters	2 black hamsters
Brand A	Brand B	Brand C	Mixed Brands A, B, C

C.

2 hamsters (any color)	2 hamsters (any color)	2 hamsters (any color)	2 hamsters (any color)
Brand A	Brand B	Brand C	Lettuce, carrots and seeds

D.

2 hamsters (any color)	2 hamsters (any color)	2 hamsters (any color)	2 hamsters (any color)
Brand A	Brand B	Brand C	Potato chips

4. At the end of one month, the class measures the hamsters' progress. Their results are contained in the following table. Which statement **best** describes their findings?

	Brand A	Brand B	Brand C
Average tooth length	0.5 cm	0.5 cm	0.6 cm
Fur condition	Good	Poor	Good
Average mass	179 grams	195 grams	175 grams
Overall energy	Moderately active	Least active	Most active

A. Brand A gives hamsters a shinier, healthier coat than the other brands.
B. Brand B makes hamsters overweight and tired.
C. Brand A is the best overall hamster food.
D. Brand C is the worst overall hamster food.

5. What mistake did the students make in compiling their data?

A. They should have measured hamster length.
B. They neglected to collect data on their control group.
C. They neglected to collect data on their experimental group.
D. They did not collect any quantitative data.

6. How should you pick up a piece of hot glassware?
   A.   with bare hands
   B.   with heat-resistant gloves or metal tongs
   C.   with the sleeve of your shirt
   D.   with a spatula

7. The biology class is asked to measure the temperature of a beaker of water. One student's thermometer reading is shown. What is the temperature reading on this thermometer?

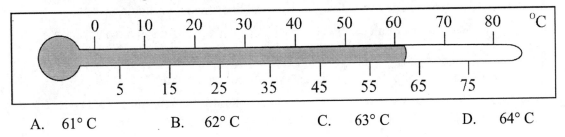

   A.   61° C   B.   62° C   C.   63° C   D.   64° C

8. What is the best estimate of the error in your reading?
   A.   1.0° C   B.   0.2° C   C.   0.1° C   D.   5.0° C

9. It seems that most of the class picked either 62° C or 63° C. Which statement best describes these answer choices?
   A.   The thermometer limited the precision of the measurement.
   B.   The thermometer limited the temperature to 63° C.
   C.   The thermometer did not limit the error in the measurement.
   D.   The thermometer is not an accurate instrument.

10. Which of the following choices converts 63° C to the correct SI unit?
    A.   63° C is already in correct SI units of Celsius.
    B.   145.4° F is in correct SI units of Fahrenheit.
    C.   336.15° K is in correct SI units of Kelvin.
    D.   273.15° K is in correct SI units of Kelvin.

11. What are the dimensions of volume?
    A.   (length)^2
    B.   (meters)^2
    C.   (length)^3
    D.   (milliliters)^3

Challenge Activity

The following issues are matters of public debate. You may have heard or read about some of these issues, while others are unfamiliar.

- the use of steroids by professional athletes
- the inclusion of evolution in school curriculums
- the development of alternative fuel sources, like ethanol or biodiesel
- the development of alternative energy sources, like landfill gas or solar power
- the establishment of school dress codes and/or uniforms
- the restriction of profanity in music and TV on public stations

Your task is to choose an issue or two and conduct an informal risk-benefit analysis. There are different ways to go about this, but here is a suggested method.

Start by sitting down with some friends at lunch and asking what they know or think about the issue. Ask your parents and other family members. Do an Internet search for terms related to the issue, and try to determine which sites describe a consensus viewpoint of the issue. Then try to figure out which ones only describe one point of view — that is, they present a **biased** viewpoint by advocating only one side. Go to the library and try to find material on your subject. Your research should generate some names of people who are experts on the issue that you are investigating. Call, write or email a few of these people to get more perspectives. Finally, write down what you have learned. An essay format is one good choice, but your teacher may want you to make a presentation or write a report. Use the space below to start jotting down ideas.

Unit 2
Physical Science

The chapters in this Unit cover the following standards:

Chapter 6:

S8P1a: Distinguish between atoms and molecules.

S8P1f: Recognize that there are more than 100 elements and some have similar properties as shown on the Periodic Table of Elements.

Chapter 7:

S8P1b: Describe the difference between pure substances (elements and compounds) and mixtures.

S8P1d: Distinguish between physical and chemical properties of matter as physical (i.e., density, melting point, boiling point) or chemical (i.e., reactivity, combustibility).

S8P1e: Distinguish between changes in matter as physical (i.e., physical change) or chemical (development of a gas, formation of precipitate and change in color).

Chapter 8:

S8P1g: Identify and demonstrate the Law of Conservation of Matter.

Chapter 9:

S8P1c: Describe the movement of particles in solid, liquid, gas and plasma states.

Chapter 10:

S8P2a: Explain energy transformation in terms of the Law of Conservation of Energy.

S8P2b: Explain the relationship between potential and kinetic energy.

S8P2c: Compare and contrast the different forms of energy (heat, light, electricity, mechanical motion, sound) and their characteristics.

Chapter 11:

S8P2d: Describe how heat can be transferred through matter by collisions of atoms (conduction) or through space (radiation). In a liquid or gas, currents will facilitate the transfer of heat (convection).

Chapter 12:

S8P3a: Determine the relationship between velocity and acceleration.

Chapter 13:

S8P3b: Demonstrate the effects of balanced and unbalanced forces on an object in terms of gravity, inertia, and friction.

S8P5a: Recognize that every object exerts gravitational force on every other object and that the force exerted depends on how much mass the objects have and how far apart they are.

Chapter 14:

S8P3c: Demonstrate the effects of simple machines (lever, inclined plane, pulley, wedge, screw and wheel and axel) on work.

Chapter 15:

S8P5c: Investigate and explain that electric currents and magnets can exert force on each other.

Chapter 16:

S8P5b: Demonstrate the advantages and disadvantages of series and parallel circuits and how they transfer energy.

Chapter 17:

S8P2a: Explain energy transformation in terms of the Law of Conservation of Energy.

S8P2c: Compare and contrast the different forms of energy (heat, light, electricity, mechanical motion, sound) and their characteristics.

S8P5b: Demonstrate the advantages and disadvantages of series and parallel circuits and how they transfer energy.

Chapter 18:

S8P4a: Identify the characteristics of electromagnetic and mechanical waves.

S8P4d: Describe how the behavior of waves is affected by medium (such as air, water, solids).

S8P4e: Relate the properties of sound to everyday experiments.

S8P4f: Diagram the parts of the wave and explain how the parts are affected by changes in amplitude and pitch.

Chapter 19:

S8P4b: Describe how the behavior of light waves is manipulated causing reflecting, refraction, diffraction and absorption.

S8P4c: Explain how the human eye sees objects and colors in terms of wavelengths.

8th Grade CRCT
SCIENCE

Chapter 6
Atoms and Elements

ELEMENTS

Ask yourself this:

Is all matter the same?

You already know the answer must be NO. There are many different kinds of matter.

Different kinds of matter are made up of atoms of *different kinds* of elements. **Elements** are substances that cannot be further broken down into simpler substances. Hydrogen is hydrogen. Gold is gold.

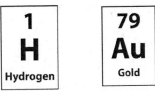

Figure 6.1 Individual Elements: Hydrogen and Gold

You are probably already familiar with many elements because most of them can be found in nature. There are 111 named elements, 90 of which are naturally-occurring. The rest have been synthesized (made) by scientists. All of these elements have a name (like hydrogen) and a **symbol** (like H).

Why so many?

Think of what the world would be like if there WEREN'T that many! The more elements there are, the more possible combinations there are. In the end, that means more different kinds of matter. How is one element different from another? The most basic answer is that each element is made up of only one kind of atom. A sample of gold is made up of only gold atoms.

THE INDIVISIBLE ATOM

Now that we've mentioned atoms, it's time to figure out what they are. To do that, look no further than the nearest pile of paper clips.

Try this:

1. Divide your pile of paper clips into two equal piles.

Figure 6.2 Pile of Paper Clips

2. Divide each of the smaller piles into two equal piles.

3. Keep dividing the piles equally until you are down to a pile containing only one paper clip. Can that one paper clip still hold papers together? YES! (Can you predict what we're going to do next? OK, read on...)

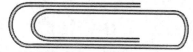

Figure 6.3 The Indivisible Paper Clip

4. Bend the paper clip in half and then make it straight again. Repeat this action until the paper clip breaks into two parts. Can half of the paper clip still hold papers together? NO!

Figure 6.4 Fragment of Paper Clip

When you get to the point where the paper clip no longer holds paper together, you can no longer call it a paper clip. If you do the same thing with any element, you will reach a point where you come to an indivisible part that has the same properties of the element, like the single paper clip. This indivisible part is called the **atom**.

But HOW are the atoms of different elements, well .. different?

Ah, yes...an excellent question! In order to describe how atoms are different from each other, you must first know the parts of the atom.

Atoms are made up of subatomic particles. The three main subatomic particles are the proton, neutron and electron. **Protons** and **neutrons** are located in the center area of the atom called a **nucleus**, and have almost all of the mass of the atom.

Electrons are located outside the nucleus. They are much tinier and move very fast. So fast, in fact, that we can usually only describe their location as a general area, instead of trying to pinpoint an exact spot. If you took a snapshot of the area around a nucleus every second for, let's say, 5 minutes, you would get a picture that looked a bit like Figure 6.5. The large dot in the middle is the nucleus. The small dots around the nucleus are the places where a single electron has shown up over the past five minutes. Those past locations define the general area where an electron is likely to be found. It is called an electron cloud, but its proper name is an **orbital**.

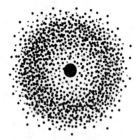

Figure 6.5 Orbital

Protons have a positive (+) charge, electrons have a negative (–) charge, and neutrons have no charge. The charge of an atom can be negative, positive or neutral. In order to be uncharged (neutral), an atom must have the same number of electrons as protons. When an atom is charged, it is called an **ion**. If there are more electrons than protons, the charge of the ion is negative. If there are fewer electrons than protons, the charge of the ion is positive. Keep in mind that the number of protons does not change under normal circumstances, but the number of electrons can and does.

With this information, we can look again at our question from the beginning of this chapter.

How are the atoms of one element different from the atoms of another element?

The atoms of each element have a different number of protons. Said another way, the protons in an atom's nucleus give it its unique identity as an element. All atoms of hydrogen (H) have one proton. All atoms of gold (Au) have 79 protons. The number of protons contained in the nucleus of each element has another name: the **atomic number**.

LOTS OF ELEMENTS ON "THE TABLE"

With over 100 different elements to choose from, how do we keep track of them all? You could say we put them "all on the table"…but in this case we don't mean where you have dinner. We mean the **Periodic Table of Elements**. (Before reading on, take a look at the next page and see if you can figure out how it is organized! Here's a hint…it's all in the numbers.)

Each rectangle on the table represents an element and contains several important pieces of information:

Element Symbol: To avoid having to write down each chemical name over and over, the Periodic Table introduces a kind of shorthand for the elements. Each element has a one-letter or two-letter abbreviation. For example, carbon is abbreviated as C. Sometimes the letters are different from what you might expect because they are abbreviations of the Latin name of the element, not the English one! This is the case with gold (Au). The symbol Au is from the Latin word for gold, "aurum."

Atomic Number: This is the number of protons in the nucleus of an atom of that element. It is also the number of electrons in an uncharged atom of the element. The atomic number is located above the element symbol.

Atomic Mass: This is the average total mass of the protons, neutrons and electrons of an atom of a specific element. The atomic mass is located below the element symbol.

You might find it odd that the Periodic Table does not specifically list the number of neutrons contained in each element's atomic nucleus. Well, it IS there…only you have to do one small calculation to find it. Subtract the atomic number (number of protons) from the atomic mass (average mass of protons, neutrons and electrons) and round your answer to the nearest whole number. CONGRATULATIONS, you have just found the number of neutrons!

The Periodic Table also tells us what KIND of matter each element is by putting them together into three general categories: metals, nonmetals and metalloids. Each of these groups is found in a specific area of the Periodic Table. Each group contains elements with similar physical properties.

GROUPING THE ELEMENTS

The Periodic Table is divided into **Groups** (sometimes called **families**). These are the vertical columns of the table. Each Group has a number. Group 1 is on the left of the table and Group 18 is on the right. Elements in the same Group have similar chemical properties, and react similarly to other elements.

Metals make up the majority of the elements on the Periodic Table, more than 75%! They are located on the left side of the table and in the center. Group 1 metals are called alkali metals. (Hydrogen is the only exception — it is a gas at room temperature and considered a nonmetal.) The **alkali metals** are

THE PERIODIC TABLE OF THE ELEMENTS

Figure 6.6 Periodic Table

Atomic Number → **36**
Symbol → **Kr**
Name → Krypton
Atomic Mass → 83.80

Noble Gases

1 IA	2 IIA	3 IIIB	4 IVB	5 VB	6 VIB	7 VIIB	8 VIIIB	9 VIIIB	10 VIIIB	11 IB	12 IIB	13 IIIA	14 IVA	15 VA	16 VIA	17 VIIA	18 VIIIA
1 H Hydrogen 1.007g																	2 He Helium 4.0026
3 Li Lithium 6.941g	4 Be Beryllium 9.01218											5 B Boron 10.81	6 C Carbon 12.011	7 N Nitrogen 14.0067	8 O Oxygen 15.9994	9 F Fluorine 18.998403	10 Ne Neon 20.179
11 Na Sodium 22.9898	12 Mg Magnesium 24.305											13 Al Aluminum 26.98154	14 Si Silicon 28.0855	15 P Phosphorus 30.97376	16 S Sulfur 32.06	17 Cl Chlorine 35.453	18 Ar Argon 39.948
19 K Potassium 39.0983	20 Ca Calcium 40.08	21 Sc Scandium 44.9559	22 Ti Titanium 47.90	23 V Vanadium 50.9415	24 Cr Chromium 51.996	25 Mn Manganese 54.9381	26 Fe Iron 55.847	27 Co Cobalt 58.9332	28 Ni Nickel 58.69	29 Cu Copper 63.546	30 Zn Zinc 65.38	31 Ga Gallium 69.723	32 Ge Germanium 72.61	33 As Arsenic 74.9216	34 Se Selenium 78.96	35 Br Bromine 79.904	36 Kr Krypton 83.80
37 Rb Rubidium 85.4678	38 Sr Strontium 87.62	39 Y Yttrium 88.9059	40 Zr Zirconium 91.22	41 Nb Niobium 92.9064	42 Mo Molybdenum 95.94	43 Tc Technetium 97.91	44 Ru Ruthenium 101.07	45 Rh Rhodium 102.9055	46 Pd Palladium 106.4	47 Ag Silver 107.868	48 Cd Cadmium 112.41	49 In Indium 114.82	50 Sn Tin 118.71	51 Sb Antimony 121.75	52 Te Tellurium 127.60	53 I Iodine 126.9045	54 Xe Xenon 131.30
55 Cs Cesium 132.9054	56 Ba Barium 137.33	57 La Lanthanum 138.9055	72 Hf Hafnium 178.49	73 Ta Tantalum 180.9479	74 W Tungsten 183.84	75 Re Rhenium 186.2	76 Os Osmium 190.2	77 Ir Iridium 192.22	78 Pt Platinum 195.09	79 Au Gold 196.9665	80 Hg Mercury 200.59	81 Tl Thallium 204.383	82 Pb Lead 207.2	83 Bi Bismuth 208.9808	84 Po Polonium 208.98244	85 At Astatine 209.98704	86 Rn Radon 222.02
87 Fr Francium 223.01976	88 Ra Radium 226.0254	89 Ac Actinium 227.02779	104 Rf Rutherfordium 261.1	105 Db Dubnium 262.11	106 Sg Seaborgium 263.12	107 Bh Bohrium 262.12	108 Hs Hassium 264.13	109 Mt Meitnerium 266.14	110 Ds Darmstadtium 271	111 Rg Roentgenium 272	112	113	114	115	116	117	118

Lanthanide Series →

58 Ce Cerium 140.12	59 Pr Praseodymium 140.9077	60 Nd Neodymium 144.24	61 Pm Promethium 144.91279	62 Sm Samarium 150.4	63 Eu Europium 151.96	64 Gd Gadolinium 157.25	65 Tb Terbium 158.9254	66 Dy Dysprosium 162.50	67 Ho Holmium 164.9304	68 Er Erbium 167.26	69 Tm Thulium 168.9342	70 Yb Ytterbium 173.04	71 Lu Lutetium 174.967

Actinide Series →

90 Th Thorium 232.0381	91 Pa Protactinium 231.0359	92 U Uranium 238.029	93 Np Neptunium 234.0482	94 Pu Plutonium 244.06424	95 Am Americium 243.06139	96 Cm Curium 247.07035	97 Bk Berkelium 247.07030	98 Cf Californium 251.0796	99 Es Einsteinium 252.08	100 Fm Fermium 257.09515	101 Md Mendelevium 258.1	102 No Nobelium 259.100	103 Lr Lawrencium 262.11

the most chemically reactive metals on the Periodic Table. Group 2 metals are called **alkaline earth metals**. The block of elements in the center of the Table (Groups 3 – 12) is called the **transition metals**. Group 13 also contains metals. Here are a few important properties of metals:

- They have metallic shine, or **luster**.
- They are usually solids at room temperature.
- They are **malleable**, meaning that they can be hammered, pounded or pressed into different shapes without breaking.
- They are **ductile**, meaning that they can be drawn into thin sheets or wires without breaking.
- They are good **conductors** of heat and electricity.

Nonmetals are on the right side of the Periodic Table in Groups 14 – 18. There are only 18 elements that fall into this category. Nonmetals are usually gases or dull, brittle solids at room temperature. Some examples of nonmetals are hydrogen (H), helium (He), carbon (C), nitrogen (N), oxygen (O), fluorine (F) and neon (Ne). Here are a few important properties of nonmetals:

- They rarely have metallic luster.
- They are usually gases at room temperature.
- Nonmetallic solids are neither malleable nor ductile.
- They are poor conductors of heat and electricity.

The **halogens** are a group of elements that are all non-metals. They are found in Group 17. The halogens react easily with many other elements. In particular, halogens chemically react with the alkali metals to form salts like NaCl (sodium chloride). Group 18 also contains non-metals. This group is called the **noble gases**. They do not usually react with any other elements; another way of saying this is that they are **inert** (a chemical property).

The elements diagonally between the metals and the nonmetals are called **metalloids**. There are 7 elements that fall into this category. These are boron (B), silicon (Si), germanium (Ge), arsenic (As), antimony (Sb), tellurium (Te) and polonium (Po). Metalloids have properties of both metals and nonmetals. One important property is that most metalloids are **semiconductors**. This means that, at certain temperatures, they conduct electricity very well; at other temperatures, they do not. Metalloids are frequently used in computer chips.

These are general categories that allow us to group elements by their physical properties. The Periodic Table may also be used to discover important information about the chemical properties of the elements. It tells us how the elements "like" to combine with other elements! This combining of atoms is called **bonding**. The process of reorganizing atoms into different bonded clusters (called **molecules)** is what happens in a **chemical reaction**. The number of protons and neutrons in a chemical reaction does not change, but the number of electrons does. We will look at chemical reactions in Chapter 8.

CHAPTER 6 REVIEW

1. Which of the following is the heaviest?

    A.   the electron   B.   the proton   C.   the neutron   D.   the nucleus

2. Neutral lithium has three protons. During a chemical reaction, one electron is removed. How many protons does lithium have now?

    A.   3

    B.   2

    C.   1

    D.   You must know what element lithium reacted with to determine this.

3. Which of the following is a positive ion?

    A.   lithium (Li), with 3 protons and 2 electrons

    B.   neon (Ne), with 10 protons and 10 electrons

    C.   oxygen (O) with 8 protons and 10 electrons

    D.   fluorine (F), with 9 protons and 10 electrons

4. Orbitals contain

    A.   thousands of fast-moving electrons.

    B.   a few fast-moving protons.

    C.   a few fast-moving electrons.

    D.   many nuclei.

5. The nucleus of an atom is

    A.   always positively charged.

    B.   always negatively charged.

    C.   always neutrally charged.

    D.   sometimes an ion charge.

1. Ⓐ Ⓑ Ⓒ Ⓓ
2. Ⓐ Ⓑ Ⓒ Ⓓ
3. Ⓐ Ⓑ Ⓒ Ⓓ
4. Ⓐ Ⓑ Ⓒ Ⓓ
5. Ⓐ Ⓑ Ⓒ Ⓓ

Vocabulary Builder

In this chapter, we discussed both general categories of matter (metal, nonmetal and metalloid) and Periodic Table groups. The elements in a Group all have similar properties. Name the specific groups we discussed and their Group number on the Periodic Table. Then do some Internet research to find out which Groups have the following traditional names: The chalcogens and the pnicogens.

Chapter 7
Properties of Matter

PROPERTIES OF MATTER

How can we tell one type of matter from another? All matter has properties that make it distinguishable from other kinds of matter. A **property** describes how matter looks, feels or interacts with other matter. To make matter easier to classify, scientists look at it in two different ways — its **physical properties** and its **chemical properties**.

A **physical property** is anything we can observe without changing the identity of the substance we are looking at. Some of the more common physical properties are: melting point, boiling point, electrical conductivity (ability to carry electrical current), thermal conductivity (ability to transfer heat), magnetism, color, odor and hardness.

Figure 7.1 Magnetism, a Physical Property

Figure 7.2 Flammability, a Chemical Property

A **chemical property** describes the way a substance may change, or react, to form other substances. Chemical properties are very different from physical properties because chemical properties describe the interaction of a substance with other matter. Here's an example: A piece of paper burns and turns into a black substance. After the flame goes out, you can no longer burn the black substance. That is because its chemical properties have been changed. Two of the most common chemical properties are: rusting (iron reacting with oxygen) and flammability (the ability of a substance to burn in the presence of oxygen).

MATTER ON THE MOVE

Matter is constantly changing. The ice in your soft drink melts, glass breaks and paper is torn apart. You're probably wondering:

What happens when matter changes?
Does it become a different kind of matter?

Let's try to answer the question by using a specific case. When you drop an ice cube into liquid water, it **melts.** This happens because the temperature of the water is higher than the temperature of the ice cube. (Imagine dumping a bag of ice on your driveway on a hot July day and you'll get the idea.) When the ice cube becomes liquid water, it is an example of a **physical change**. The solid water turned to liquid water. It doesn't turn into oil or potato chips…it remains water. A physical change may have occurred if a substance changes **color, size, shape** or **temperature**. The state (or physical form) of the substance may also change as you'll see in Chapter 9.

Chemical changes happen when one substance is changed to become another substance. If it could happen, ice cubes changing into potato chips would be an example of a chemical change. More realistic examples of chemical changes would be cooking a raw egg, milk spoiling or food digesting. Milk needs to be in the refrigerator or else it will go sour. When it is left out, the milk gets a sour odor and becomes lumpy. (If you've ever seen or smelled spoiled milk…you'll understand.) Unlike physical changes, you usually cannot reverse chemical changes. You can melt ice to get water and freeze that water to get ice again…but you can't "unspoil" milk! To identify a chemical change look for observable signs such as **color change, bubbling and fizzing, light production, smoke and the presence of heat**.

Physical and chemical *properties* are ways that scientists classify different types of matter. Physical and chemical *changes* are things that happen to matter to change it from one form to another. Matter can be physically combined to form **mixtures**. It can also be chemically combined to form **compounds**. Figure 7.3 should help you to visualize this.

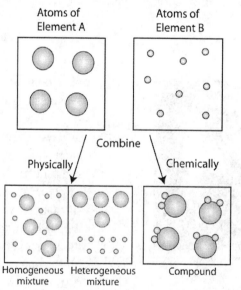

Figure 7.3 Atoms Can Combine Physically and Chemically

Each form of matter shown in Figure 7.3 has its own characteristics, which we will look at now.

MIXTURES

A mixture results when two or more substances (either elements or compounds) combine <u>physically</u>. That simply means that the two substances can be side by side *without changing*. Another way of stating this is that, in a mixture, both substances keep their individual properties. A mixture can usually be separated back into its individual substances. Let's say we were to put a teaspoon of salt and a teaspoon of pepper in a plastic bag, and then shake the bag (AFTER it has been sealed, of course). The result would be a mixture of salt and pepper. The two substances are together, yet they still retain their original properties.

Here's another example. When salt is dissolved into water, it creates a **solution**, which is a liquid mixture. If you drink the salt water, you can taste the salt in the water. The salt is still "salty," and the water is still a liquid, so these substances have not changed chemically. The salt and water can be separated by evaporation (if you wanted to wait that long). When the water vapor evaporates, the salt will be left behind.

There are two kinds of mixtures: homogeneous and heterogeneous.

Homogeneous mixtures are mixtures that have a uniform (the same) composition and appearance throughout. If a spoonful of sugar is dissolved in a glass of water, the solution is the same throughout the entire glass. Any sample taken from the glass would have the same combination of water and sugar!

Figure 7.4 Homogeneous

Heterogeneous mixtures are mixtures that do <u>not</u> have uniform composition and appearance throughout. The individual components stay physically separated (not chemically combined) and can be seen as separate components. If you put a spoonful of sand into a glass of water, even after stirring it or shaking it, the sand will settle to the bottom of the glass. Any sample you took from the glass would have a different combination of water and sand, and since the sand would settle to the bottom, you could end up with mostly one or the other! More examples of heterogeneous mixtures are oil and vinegar salad dressing, paint, blood and soil.

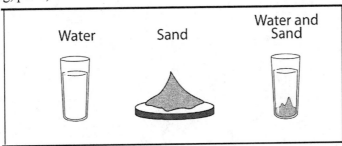

Figure 7.5 Heterogeneous

PURE SUBSTANCES

A **pure substance** is a type of matter that has its own unique set of chemical and physical properties. To find out if a substance is a pure substance, ask yourself this:

Can the substance be *physically* broken down into any more parts?

If the answer is "no," then you have a pure substance. Pure substances can be elements (which we've covered) or compounds.

COMPOUNDS

When atoms of two or more elements combine chemically, they form a **compound**. This new compound has completely different properties than the individual elements from which it is made. Think about this: hydrogen and oxygen are VERY flammable gases when in their most basic, elemental form. But when we put them together, they form water... which we all know is so stable it is used to *put out* fires. Not only has the chemical property of flammability changed, the physical property of state has also: the two *gases* form a liquid.

Remember that the smallest unit of an element is an atom? In a similar way, the smallest unit of a compound is a **molecule**. One molecule of water consists of two atoms of hydrogen (H) and one atom of oxygen (O). The **chemical formula** that describes each molecule of water is H_2O.

A compound cannot be *physically separated* into its individual components. You cannot, for instance, beat water with a stick to break it back down to hydrogen and oxygen. It can, however, be *chemically* separated.

Compounds may also be *physically combined* with other compounds to form mixtures, as shown in Table 7.1.

Table 7.1 Interactions of Matter

Elements (symbol)	Compounds (chemical formula)	Heterogeneous Mixtures	Homogeneous Mixtures
sodium (Na) chlorine (Cl)	table salt (NaCl)	salt and sawdust	salt and water
carbon (C) oxygen (O) hydrogen (H)	sugar ($C_{12}H_{22}O_{11}$) water (H_2O)	sugar and graphite water and graphite	sugar and water
oxygen (O) hydrogen (H) carbon (C)	water (H_2O) alcohol (CH_3OH)	oil and water oil and alcohol iron filings and alcohol	water and alcohol
nitrogen (N) oxygen (O) hydrogen (H)	ammonia (NH_3) nitric acid (HNO_3)	polluted air (contains dust and dirt, as well as nitric acid)	ammonia and water filtered air (gas only)

As we will see in Chapter 8, compounds can also be *chemically separated* or *combined* in processes called **chemical reactions**.

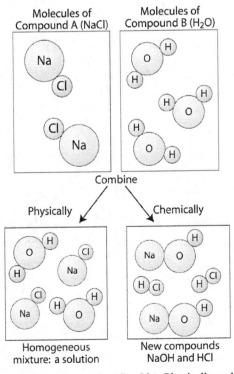

Figure 7.6 Molecules Can Combine Physically and Chemically

CHAPTER 7 REVIEW

1. Marquis is studying an unknown substance. He has recorded several properties in his note-book. Which of these properties is a physical property?

   A. boiling point
   B. flammability

   C. tendency to tarnish
   D. tendency to rust

2. The melting point describes the transition from a

   A. liquid to a solid.
   B. liquid to a gas.

   C. solid to a gas.
   D. solid to a liquid.

3. The chemical combination of Atom A and Atom B would result in

   A. an atom AB.
   B. an element AB.

   C. a molecule AB.
   D. a nucleus AB.

4. A homogeneous mixture could be described as

   A. a pure substance.
   B. evenly mixed.

   C. chemically bound.
   D. unevenly mixed.

5. What does the following figure show?

   A. a homogenous mixture
   B. a heterogeneous mixture

   C. a heterogeneous compound
   D. a solution

1. Ⓐ	Ⓑ	Ⓒ	Ⓓ
2. Ⓐ	Ⓑ	Ⓒ	Ⓓ
3. Ⓐ	Ⓑ	Ⓒ	Ⓓ
4. Ⓐ	Ⓑ	Ⓒ	Ⓓ
5. Ⓐ	Ⓑ	Ⓒ	Ⓓ

Chapter 8
Chemical Reactions

The Law of Conservation of Mass states that, in a chemical reaction, there is no loss of mass. This means you end up with as many atoms of each element at the end of a chemical reaction as you had before the reaction took place. Nothing is gained. Nothing is lost. The organization of the atoms (what is, and is not, bonded together) simply changes.

If you think back to Chapter 7, you'll realize that you already discovered this! Recall that sometimes elements join together to become **compounds**, sometimes compounds break down to their individual elements, and sometimes there's a combination of both. Most of the materials we come into contact with are compounds. A single "particle" of a compound is called a **molecule**.

DESCRIBING REACTIONS

In a chemical reaction, we call the materials that are going to react (be reorganized) **reactants**. The materials that result from the reaction are called the **product**. There will be the same amount of each type of element before the reaction as after the reaction. To demonstrate this, let's take a look at a molecule you are very familiar with: water.

As you know, the chemical formula for water is H_2O. All "H_2O" means is that you have two atoms of hydrogen (H), chemically bound to one atom of oxygen (O). If we were to look at this combination as a mathematical equation, it might look like Equation 8.1.

$$H + H + O = HHO \qquad \textbf{Equation 8.1}$$

If we look at this as a **chemical equation**, we write it a little differently, adding **coefficients** to the atomic symbols. The coefficients tell us how many of each kind of atom there are. If an element is represented by only one atom, there is no need to write in a coefficient of 1. So, two atoms of hydrogen react with one atom of oxygen to form one molecule of water as follows:

$$2H + O \longrightarrow H_2O \qquad \textbf{Equation 8.2}$$

The arrow tells you that something happens to one set of atoms that results in their reorganization into something else. On the left side of the arrow are the reactants, and on the right side are the products.

Challenge Question:

After the chemical reaction in Equation 8.2, you find that you have 10 grams of water. How much oxygen and hydrogen did you have before the reaction?

Remember that the product of a chemical reaction may have some physical properties similar to the physical properties of the reactants, but it will ALWAYS have different chemical properties. This is because the product has a different arrangement of atoms than the reactants.

REACTION RATE

The **rate** of a reaction describes how fast or slow the reaction proceeds. The rate of the reaction depends on several factors, including temperature and surface area of the reactants. Increasing these will increase the amount of interaction between atoms, which will then increase the rate of the overall reaction.

How does raising the temperature of reactants speed up a reaction?

When two chemicals react, their molecules have to collide with each other with enough energy for the reaction to take place. By raising the temperature, you raise the energy levels of the molecules in the reaction…and speed up the rate of the reaction!

How does raising the surface area of the reactants speed up the reaction?

Let's look at an actual chemical reaction to demonstrate the answer. When you make a fire, you start out with tiny pieces of tinder, like pine needles and leaves. These are then used to light kindling, like small branches and twigs. Finally, a mature fire is made by adding logs. The point is to start the fire with low-bulk, high-surface area materials, which will undergo a chemical change (burning) quickly. Left alone, a tinder fire will quickly burn out. So, at each of the next steps, higher-bulk, lower-surface area materials (like kindling, then logs) are added. Decreasing the surface area slows the reaction, so you get a slow-burning fire.

Figure 8.1 Three Stages of a Fire

It may be hard for you to see burning as a chemical reaction, but it is. Let's look at another burning reaction and see if this concept makes more sense. Many hikers and campers carry solid bars of magnesium. They do this because magnesium is a **pyrophoric** metal — it will ignite (burn) in air at temperatures below room temperature.

So, how do the hikers carry it?

Excellent question! Magnesium in block form — about the size of a bar of soap — is very difficult to ignite and quite safe to carry. When you want a fire, you make camp and shave off some thin slivers from the bar, to use as kindling. By doing this, you have *increased the surface area* of the reactant magnesium and also the rate of its reaction with oxygen. The result is a white-hot flame.

Figure 8.2 Shaving Magnesium

ENERGY IN CHEMICAL REACTIONS

During chemical reactions, chemical bonds in the reactants break and the molecules rearrange themselves into the products. The chemicals only react if their molecules collide with enough energy for a reaction to take place. So, to determine if a reaction is going to take place under the given conditions, you need to know which side has more energy. Scientists do this by dividing reactions into two categories: exothermic and endothermic reactions.

If the chemical energy of the reactants is more than the chemical energy of the products, then the energy difference is given off during the reaction. These kinds of reactions are called **exothermic reactions**. Why? The reason can be found in the term itself. *Exo* is a prefix that means "to go out" or "exit," and *thermic* can mean "heat" or "energy." So, in an exothermic reaction, "heat goes out."

Think of it like this:

Figure 8.3 Exothermic Reaction

This energy difference is given off in different forms, such as light energy (like in a light stick), electrical energy (like a dry cell battery) or heat energy (like a campfire).

If the chemical energy of the reactants is less than the chemical energy of the products, energy must be absorbed to make the reaction occur. A chemical reaction where energy is absorbed is called an **endothermic reaction**. *Endo* means "to go in" (and you already know what *thermic* means). In an endothermic reaction, "heat goes in."

$$\text{Reactant} + \text{Energy} \longrightarrow \text{Product}$$

Figure 8.4 Endothermic Reaction

The energy added to the system is often in the form of thermal energy, as when you are cooking food. In many cases, it is light energy. An example of this is the energy that plants use from the Sun to make their own food in the process of photosynthesis.

It is important to point out that, even though we refer to energy as being lost or gained, energy is just like matter: *it is not created or destroyed*. The overall amount of energy stays the same, even when the energy involved changes forms from electrical to light to heat. **The Law of Conservation of Energy** puts all this into one neat package by stating that energy is neither created nor destroyed. We'll talk more about this Law in Chapter 10.

CHAPTER 8 REVIEW

1. What does the phrase "the reorganization of reactants into products" describe?

   A.   a physical reaction

   B.   a chemical reaction

   C.   a chemical formula

   D.   an element

2. Coal is made of carbon. Coal burns at high temperatures in the presence of oxygen. The result of this chemical reaction is

   A.   more of the same coal.

   B.   coal with different physical properties.

   C.   a new chemical compound.

   D.   the creation of new elements.

Use the following chemical reaction to answer questions 3 – 5:

$$SO_2 + H_2O \longrightarrow H^+ + HSO_3^-$$

3. How many atoms of reactant are there?

   A.   2   B.   4   C.   6   D.   12

4. Gillian mixes 5 grams of sulfur dioxide (SO_2) with 6 grams of water, in a 10-gram, stoppered test tube. After the reaction, she weighs the test tube and its contents. What product mass ($H^+ + HSO_3^-$) does she record in her laboratory report?

   A.   5 g

   B.   6 g

   C.   11 g

   D.   21 g

5. The Law of Conservation of Mass states that which of the following will always be equal before and after a chemical reaction?

   A.   the number of atoms of product and atoms of reactant

   B.   the number of molecules of product and molecules of reactant

   C.   density of the reactants

   D.   the surface area of the product and the reactant

1. Ⓐ Ⓑ Ⓒ Ⓓ
2. Ⓐ Ⓑ Ⓒ Ⓓ
3. Ⓐ Ⓑ Ⓒ Ⓓ
4. Ⓐ Ⓑ Ⓒ Ⓓ
5. Ⓐ Ⓑ Ⓒ Ⓓ

Chapter 9
States of Matter

Have you ever looked at a pot of boiling water? The water is a liquid, but the bubbles are a gas. And how about this: have you ever seen a half-frozen ice cube with water trapped in ice pockets? Here we have a solid (ice) that is surrounding the liquid water.

Water can be found in solid, liquid and gas forms. How does that happen?

Solid, liquid and gas are the names of different physical forms of matter, or **phases**. These are called **states of matter**.

- **Solids** are made of closely-packed atoms or molecules, and maintain a rigid form without a container. Solids are **incompressible**, meaning that they cannot be "squeezed" down to a smaller size.

- **Liquids** are made of closely associated atoms or molecules, and will flow to conform to the shape of a container. Liquids are **mostly incompressible**.

- **Gases** are made of mostly unassociated atoms or molecules, and will expand to fill a container. Gases are **compressible**, meaning that their volume can be reduced by applying force.

Solids are formed when the attractive forces between atoms are greater than the energy causing them to move apart. The atoms are locked in position near each other. Sometimes they are in very fixed, structured positions; this is referred to as a **crystalline solid**. Examples are salt, diamond, quartz and ice.

Figure 9.1 Crystalline Solids

Other times, the solid has no structure to it; these are **amorphous solids**. Examples are wax and many foods, like cotton candy.

Figure 9.2 Amorphous Solids

So, in the solid phase, the atoms cannot move past one another. You might think this means there is no motion at all, but that is not so! Each atom still has energy associated with it, so it must move. In fact, atoms in the solid phase vibrate. You can think of them as small children that have been told to sit in a chair; since they cannot get up, they squirm around in place.

As the temperature of a solid increases, the amount of vibration increases. The solid will keep its shape until the amount of energy added is greater than the attractive forces between the atoms. Now the atoms start to move, forming a liquid.

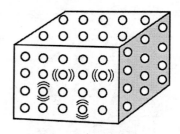

Particles can vibrate, but remain in fixed positions, with strong association between them.

Figure 9.3 Particle Motion in Solids

Challenge Question

The temperature at which a solid becomes a liquid is called its:

_____

In **liquids**, atoms can move past one another and bump into each other. This is why liquids can "flow" to take the shape of their container. However, they still remain relatively close to each other, like solids. As the temperature (and motion of the atoms) of a liquid is increased, the amount of movement of individual atoms increases. They bump into each other with increasing thermal energy. Eventually, some particles have enough energy to "escape." These atoms have entered the gas phase.

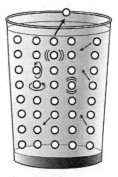

Particles can vibrate, rotate and translate. Particles are not fixed, but do associate with one another.

Figure 9.4 Particle Motion in Liquids

Challenge Question

The temperature at which a liquid becomes a gas is called its:

_____

Atoms and molecules in the gas phase have little interaction with each other, beyond occasionally bumping into one another. **Gases** have a low density — that is, there are few particles occupying a given space. Increasing the temperature of a gas increases the movement of the gas particles. If they are placed in a container at fixed volume, this increased movement will cause them to hit the walls of that container with greater frequency and greater force. This creates increased **pressure**.

From this discussion, you have seen that increasing the **thermal energy** of a given material increases the motion of the atoms or molecules of the material. This is summed up in Figure 9.6.

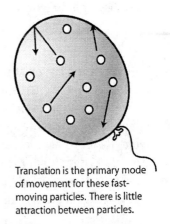

Translation is the primary mode of movement for these fast-moving particles. There is little attraction between particles.

Figure 9.5 Particle Motion in Gases

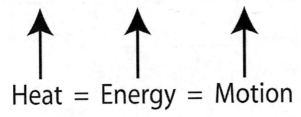

Heat = Energy = Motion

Figure 9.6 Energy Trends

PHASE TRANSITIONS

The transformation of matter from one state to another is called a **phase transition**. Phase transitions occur at very precise points, when the energy of motion (measured as temperature) in the atoms is too much or too little for the atom to remain in that state.

Phase transitions are explained in Table 9.1 and Figure 9.7.

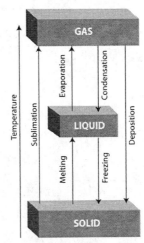

Figure 9.7 Phase Transitions Illustrated

Table 9.1 Phase Transitions Described

Phase Transition	Description
Melting	Solid to Liquid
Evaporation	Liquid to Gas
Sublimation	Solid to Gas (skipping Liquid)
Condensation	Gas to Liquid
Freezing	Liquid to Solid
Deposition	Gas to Solid (skipping Liquid)

At the beginning of this chapter, we looked at the transition from the liquid to the gas phase and from the solid to liquid phase. Now, let's look back at our old friend WATER, and examine its phase changes more closely.

Liquid water can exist in a range of temperatures. Cold drinking water may be around 4°C. Hot shower water has more energy, and it may be around 40°C. However, at 100°C, water will begin to undergo a phase transition from liquid to gas. At this point, (at least for a little while) the energy added to the liquid will not go into increasing the temperature. Instead, it will be used to send molecules of water into the gas state. So, no matter how high the flame is on the stove, a pot of boiling water will remain at 100°C until all of the water has undergone transition to the gas phase! Said another way, turning up the stovetop heat will *accelerate* the liquid-to-gas transition, but it will not change the temperature of the water. Figure 9.8 illustrates how this works.

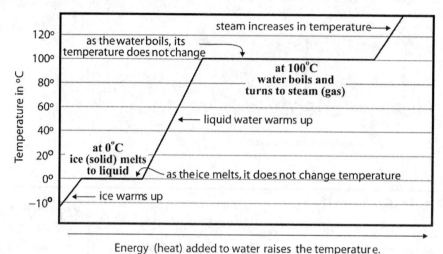

Figure 9.8 Phase Transitions of Water

This same process can be seen in reverse if we simply look at Figure 9.8, starting on the right side and moving left. You try it!

Challenge Activity

Use Figure 9.8 to describe the transition of water from the gas phase (steam) to the liquid phase (water).

_____

_____

_____

What about the pot of boiling water we mentioned at the beginning of the chapter? Well, have you ever thought about WHERE the bubbles come from? The energy (heat) introduced at the bottom of the pot causes a phase transition of liquid water to the gaseous state at the *bottom of the pan*. Because gases are less dense than liquids, the gas forms pockets (bubbles) of gas, which rise to the surface of the water and burst. Isn't science awesome? However, one mystery still remains…even with all we know about states of matter, we still are unable predict *where* the individual bubbles will form. Hmm.

Activity: Phase Transitions	
The following processes are phase transitions. In the space provided, write what they are.	
Water droplets coat your cold soda can on a hot day.	
A cloud releases rain.	
Solid dry ice steams in air.	
Glaciers floating in the ocean are shrinking. ·	
Morning dew disappears from the grass by midday.	
A cloud releases snow.	

Molecular Motion Activity

1. **Place two clear glass beakers on a heat-resistant surface.**

2. **Fill the first beaker with water at room temperature.**

3. **Fill the second beaker with hot water (be careful when handling hot water!).**

4. **Place five drops of food coloring into both beakers and observe the difference in how the coloring spreads throughout the water.**

Observations:

You should see the coloring spread slowly in the beaker with room temperature water and much more rapidly in the hot water.

Conclusions:

The atoms in the hot water are MOVING much faster than the atoms in the room temperature water. When the atoms move faster, they move around the food coloring!

CHAPTER 9 REVIEW

The figure to the right shows the three phases of a material, X, in a closed container. Use it to answer questions 1 and 2.

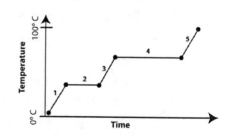

1. Which phase has the greatest density?

    A.   the solid phase
    B.   the liquid phase
    C.   the gas phase
    D.   The temperature must be known to answer this question.

2. Tina uses a vice to squeeze each container. Which turns out to be the most compressible?

    A.   the solid phase container
    B.   the liquid phase container
    C.   the gas phase container
    D.   The temperature must be known to answer this question.

3. How does perspiration cool your skin?

    A.   It carries heat off when it condenses on your skin.
    B.   It carries heat off when it evaporates from your skin.
    C.   It carries heat off when it sublimes from your skin.
    D.   It carries heat off when it deposits on your skin.

The figure shows the phase transition of water. Use it to answer questions 4 and 5.

4. During which period(s) of time is water in the liquid phase?

    A.   2   C.   3
    B.   2 and 3   D.   3 and 4

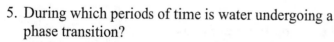

5. During which periods of time is water undergoing a phase transition?

    A.   1 and 3   C.   2, 3 and 4
    B.   1, 3 and 5   D.   2 and 4

Vocabulary Builder

In this chapter, we talked about how atoms move in the various states of matter, using the terms vibrate, rotate and translate. Based on this discussion, define these terms, (you may need the help of a dictionary, but try to define the word first without one.) Discuss how the common definition of translation (related to language) is similar to the less-common definition of translation (related to motion).

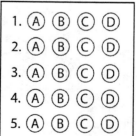

1. (A) (B) (C) (D)
2. (A) (B) (C) (D)
3. (A) (B) (C) (D)
4. (A) (B) (C) (D)
5. (A) (B) (C) (D)

Chapter 10
Energy

CONSERVATION OF ENERGY

You have heard the term "conservation of energy" before. It is usually used to describe the effort to *save* energy, like when your parents tell you "turn off the lights when you leave the room!" Coaches are saying the same thing to an athlete when they tell her to "slow down and conserve your energy for the end of the race."

When scientists talk about **conservation of energy**, they are talking about something a little different. They are talking about an important characteristic of energy.

Energy may be transformed (changed) from one form to another, but in the end, you always end up with as much energy as you started with.

It may not be the same kinds of energy. Some of it may even have escaped the area that it started in. But the total amount of energy remains the same. This characteristic is often stated as the **Law of Conservation of Energy**, which simply says that energy can neither be created nor destroyed. When we use energy, it doesn't disappear. We change it from one form into another.

FORMS OF ENERGY

Energy can be found in many different forms. Some examples of different forms of energy are light, heat, sound and motion. Any of these may transform. It is called an energy **transition**. For example, a car engine burns gasoline, converting the chemical energy in gasoline into mechanical energy that makes the car move. Although there are many forms of energy, they can all be put into two general categories: **kinetic energy** and **potential energy**.

Kinetic energy is energy of motion. The kinetic energy of an object is the energy it possesses because of its motion. To put it another way, it's energy that has the ability (because of its motion) to act on something else and move it somewhere.

When we think of the word "potential" we usually think about how something or someone *could* do something *if* certain things happened. For instance, have you ever heard something like this:

Albert plays baseball so well — what potential!

or how about this:

Stop playing video games! You are wasting your potential!

Well potential energy is not exactly about your future. It's more about the future of an energy source. The term **potential energy** means the stored energy in an object due to its position or composition. In other words, the object *could* exert this energy *if* something happened. Let's look, for example, at what happens when an archer pulls the string of a bow backward with an arrow. The more the string is stretched backward, the more potential energy is stored. All that has to happen to convert the **potential energy** in the bow into **kinetic energy** is for the archer to let go!

Let's take a closer look at some forms of kinetic and potential energy.

KINETIC ENERGY

Figure 10.1 Mechanical Energy

Mechanical Energy is the energy an object has due to its motion. This kind of energy allows one object to apply a force to another object and make it move.

In Figure 10.1, a naughty cat is applying a force by swatting a vase. The cat is using mechanical energy.

Electrical Energy is energy resulting from the movement of electrical charges. Recall that atoms are made of sub-atomic particles called electrons, protons and neutrons. Applying a force (like friction or voltage) can make some of the electrons move from atom to atom. The movement of these electrons is called electricity. Static electricity and lightning are examples of electrical energy.

Figure 10.2 Electrical Energy

Figure 10.3 Radiant Energy

Radiant Energy is energy that travels in electromagnetic waves, like that of the Sun. In a vacuum, like space, electromagnetic radiation moves at a speed of 3.0×10^8 m/s. Since that is a very high speed, you can infer that electromagnetic radiation carries with it a lot of energy. It does. After all, the Sun heats our whole planet with its radiant energy! Other examples of radiant energy are visible light, X-rays, gamma rays and radio waves.

Thermal Energy is the internal energy in substances. Think of this as the movement of the atoms and molecules within a substance. This movement often generates heat, which is why thermal energy is thought of as heat energy. Thermal energy always moves from hot (high energy) to cold (low energy). We will discuss this more in Chapter 11.

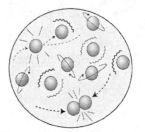

Figure 10.4 Thermal Energy

Sound Energy is the movement of energy through substances in compression waves (waves that have to travel through a medium, like air or water). Sound is produced when a force causes an object or substance to vibrate. When this happens, the energy is transferred through the substance in a wave. Sound moves more quickly in denser materials (like solids) than in less dense materials (like gases).

Figure 10.5 Sound Energy

POTENTIAL ENERGY

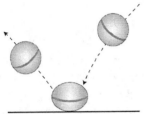

Elastic Energy is the energy stored in elastic materials as the result of their stretching or compressing. Elastic potential energy can be stored in rubber bands, bungee chords, trampolines, springs, an arrow drawn into a bow, etc.

Figure 10.6 Elastic Energy

Chemical Energy is energy stored in the bonds of atoms and molecules. It is the energy that holds these particles together. Oil, natural gas and propane all have stored chemical energy. Humans harness this energy by burning these materials. Batteries are another example.

Figure 10.7 Chemical Energy

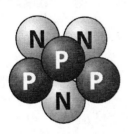

Figure 10.8 Nuclear Energy

Nuclear Energy is energy stored in the nucleus of an atom. It is the energy that holds the nucleus together. It is released when a nucleus is split apart, or when more than one nuclei are combined. Nuclear power plants split the nuclei of uranium atoms in a process called **fission**. The Sun combines the nuclei of hydrogen atoms in a process called **fusion**. Scientists are working on creating nuclear fusion energy on Earth, because the energy put out by a fusion power plant would be much greater than the nuclear fission power plants we have today.

Gravitational Energy is the energy of position or place. For instance, if you saw a boulder resting at the top of a mountain, it would contain a great deal of gravitational potential energy. When water is held behind a dam in a hydropower plant, it has a great deal of gravitational potential energy...all that it would take for the potential energy to be converted into kinetic energy is for the dam gates to open.

Figure 10.9 Gravitation Energy

KINETIC AND POTENTIAL ENERGY CONVERSION

Think back to the early chapters of this book when we first made you aware that you had been a scientist practically your whole life. The example we looked at was when you threw a ball downward with varying amounts of force to see how it affected the height of the resulting bounce. Now that you have that image in your head, think of what happened to the ball when it first hit the ground.

1 You threw the ball down.

2 It hit the ground.

3 The ball sprang up from the ground, launched into the air.

4 At its maximum bounce height, the ball reversed direction and began to fall.

5 The ball fell toward the ground.

Here is what happened in scientific terms. After the ball left your hand in step **(1)**, it was moving, so it had kinetic (mechanical) energy. When it hit the ground in step **(2)**, it got flattened out, or smashed (although, as scientists, we should use the technical term that the ball **deformed**). You can see this in Figure 10.6. This deformation resulted in the ball acquiring stored (elastic) energy. It then bounced in step **(3)**. As it traveled upward, it again had kinetic (mechanical) energy. Eventually, it slowed down, in step **(4)**. At this point, the kinetic energy was being converted into potential (gravitational) energy. When the ball reached the peak of its journey upward, for a split second all of the kinetic energy was converted into potential energy. As the ball fell back down toward the ground in step **(5)**, the potential energy was gradually converted into kinetic (mechanical) energy. The closer the ball got to the ground, the less potential energy and the more kinetic energy it had. Each time the ball bounced this process would repeat itself.

THERMAL ENERGY LOSS

Energy conversion from one form to another happens constantly. It is happening in every move you make and every electrical appliance you turn on. But energy transfer is not efficient. That means that some energy is "lost" during nearly every transition. But its not really "lost", it is actually just a side conversion into thermal energy. Thermal energy is often the result of **friction** (that is, things rubbing against each other). Table 10.1 shows some examples. We will take a closer look at thermal energy in the next chapter.

Table10.1 Common Energy Changes

Use of Energy	Resultant Change in Energy	Energy Lost As
turning on a battery-powered flashlight	chemical to electrical to light	heat from flashlight bulb
turning the turbine in an electric generator	mechanical to electrical	heat from friction within the generator
turning on a light bulb	electrical to light	heat from bulb
using a nuclear reaction to produce heat	nuclear to thermal	heat from reaction
rock rolling down a hill	potential to kinetic	heat from friction of rock against earth

Activity

Write the appropriate energy transition in the space provided.

_____

_____

_____

_____

Activity

Read the following scenarios, and determine what kind of energy transition is being described.

Example: Maurice applies the brakes to slow his bike.

Answer: Applying the brake introduces friction, which helps Maurice convert the mechanical, kinetic energy of motion to thermal energy at the point of contact between the brake and the bike wheel.

1. A cornstalk grows 3 inches in one day.

2. Susan lights a candle.

3. The Mars Rovers are powered by solar cells.

4. The Sun is a giant fusion reactor.

5. Tanya talks on the telephone to Olivia.

CHAPTER 10 REVIEW

1. Beating a drum represents what kind of energy conversion?
   - A. electrical to mechanical
   - B. mechanical to sound
   - C. chemical to electrical
   - D. sound to heat

2. A car uses gasoline for fuel. Which of the following describes the energy conversion from gasoline to the movement of the car?
   - A. mechanical to electrical
   - B. heat to light
   - C. electrical to nuclear
   - D. chemical to mechanical

3. Which of the following is an example of electrical energy being converted to light energy?
   - A. ringing a doorbell
   - B. striking a match
   - C. turning on a computer monitor
   - D. water falling over a dam

4. Which of the following uses mechanical energy to function?
   - A. computer
   - B. battery
   - C. microwave oven
   - D. windmill

5. An engine converts 95% of energy input into useful work output. What happens to the remaining 5% of the energy?
   - A. It is converted to heat or to some other form of unusable energy.
   - B. It is destroyed in the process of converting from one type of energy to another.
   - C. It is stored in the engine for later use.
   - D. It is lost along with the mass of the fuel.

Vocabulary Builder

One type of energy we discussed in this chapter is elastic energy. Based on that brief discussion, write a definition of the term "elastic collision." (HINT: Think of this in terms of conserving kinetic energy.) Then define "inelastic collision."

Find an example of each.

---

1. Ⓐ Ⓑ Ⓒ Ⓓ
2. Ⓐ Ⓑ Ⓒ Ⓓ
3. Ⓐ Ⓑ Ⓒ Ⓓ
4. Ⓐ Ⓑ Ⓒ Ⓓ
5. Ⓐ Ⓑ Ⓒ Ⓓ

Chapter 11
Thermal Energy

As you know, all matter is made of particles. We investigated atoms and groups of atoms (called molecules) earlier in this book. One additional piece of information you need about atoms and molecules is that they are in constant motion. From what you learned about potential and kinetic energy, the fact that atoms and molecules are in motion should indicate to you that they have kinetic energy. The faster the particles move, the more kinetic energy you can infer they have. The measure of how much kinetic energy is in a substance is called its **temperature**. That doesn't mean that every part of an object has the same exact temperature, or that every atom of an object has the same amount of kinetic energy as every other atom. An object's temperature is the **average kinetic energy** of all the atoms in the object.

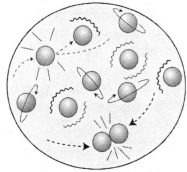

Figure 11.1 Atomic Motion

HEATING UP

When you hear the word heat, you probably think of things that feel hot to the touch. But heat has just as much to do with things that feel cold. A scientific definition for heat is the transfer of energy between objects that are at different temperatures. So why do some things feel hot and others cold? When two objects at different temperatures come in contact with one another, energy is always transferred from the object with a higher temperature to the object with a lower temperature. When you touch an object that feels cold, what is actually happening is that you are transferring energy from your fingers into the object. This is because your fingers have a higher temperature.

So **heat** is the transfer of **thermal energy**. There are three main processes through which thermal energy is transferred: conduction, convection and radiation.

Figure 11.2 Modes of Heat Transfer

If both objects are at the same temperature, then no heat will be transferred when they come in contact with each other. This situation is called **thermal equilibrium**.

CONDUCTION

Conduction is the transfer of energy through matter, from particle to particle. When substances come in contact with one another, their particles collide and thermal energy is transferred from the higher temperature substance to the lower temperature substance. Conduction makes some particles slow down, and other particles speed up, until all particles have the same average kinetic energy. This interaction takes place until all particles in both substances have the same temperature... thermal equilibrium. You have probably experienced conduction before. For example, you have probably stirred hot soup with a metal spoon until you started to feel the heat from the hot water conducting through the spoon to your fingers. Ouch!

Substances that transfer thermal energy easily are called **conductors**. Substances that do not transfer thermal energy easily are called **insulators**. When you open a can of soda and want to keep it cold, sometimes you put it in a foam sleeve. The foam around the can acts as an insulator and keeps the heat energy of the room from transferring into the can.

> **Challenge Question**
>
> A cold soda is left out on the counter on a warm day. After a few minutes, water droplets cover the surface of the can. Explain why this happens and name the phase change.

CONVECTION

What happens when you boil a pot of water? You have probably observed that when water boils, it bubbles in a circular pattern in the pot. This circular pattern happens because of **convection**. **Convection** is the transfer of thermal energy by the movement of a liquid or a gas. The water at the bottom of the pot gets hot because it comes in contact with the heated metal... conduction. When this water gets heated it becomes less dense, because particles have absorbed energy and spread apart. The warmer water rises through the denser (cooler) water above it. Once it reaches the surface, the warm water begins to cool and eventually sinks back toward the bottom of the pot. This whole sequence has a circular motion and is called a **convection current**.

RADIATION

Radiation is different from conduction and convection because it doesn't have to involve energy transfer between particles of matter. Radiation is the transfer of energy through *matter or space* as electromagnetic waves (which you will learn more about in Chapter 18). All objects radiate electromagnetic waves, but our largest, most important source of these, as you know, is the Sun. Solar radiation is the essential source of energy to all life on Earth, because it provides the energy needed for plant photosynthesis (the process where plants make their own food, using sunlight as the energy source). Without sunlight, there would be no photosynthesis, which means there would be no plants. Without plants and the heat of the Sun, there would be no animals (like us) that eat plants!

HEAT, TEMPERATURE AND THERMAL ENERGY...THE DIFFERENCE

It's now time to review an important distinction. Although heat, temperature and thermal energy are related to one another, they are not the same thing. Heat is a transfer of thermal energy, or the amount of energy transferred from one object to another. Temperature is the average kinetic energy of an object's particles. Thermal energy is the total energy of those particles. While thermal energy varies with the mass of the object, temperature does not. The table below should help you remember the differences among these terms.

Table 11.1 Difference in Heat Lingo

Temperature	Thermal Energy	Heat
A measure of the average energy of the particles in a substance	The total energy of the particles in a substance	The transfer of energy between objects that are at different temperatures

CHAPTER 11 REVIEW

1. Francisco was heating soup in a metal pan on the stove. He noticed that the soup was about to boil over. He quickly grabbed the handle of the pan to remove it from the heat. Just as quickly, he let go of the pan because he burned his hand. What kind of heat transfer occurred through the metal handle of the pan?

    A.   radiation   C.   conduction

    B.   convection   D.   insulation

2. Which of the following processes gives off more energy than it absorbs?

    A.   melting ice

    B.   burning propane in a gas heater

    C.   sublimation of carbon dioxide ice to carbon dioxide gas

    D.   recharging a car battery

3. How does the energy from the Sun reach the Earth?

    A.   conduction   C.   radiation

    B.   convection   D.   thermal convection

4. Which of the following specifically describes the transfer of energy?

    A.   heat

    B.   temperature

    C.   average kinetic energy

    D.   thermal energy

5. A material that does **not** conduct thermal energy easily is a(n)

    A.   conductor.   C.   radiator.

    B.   metal.   D.   insulator.

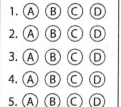

Chapter 12
Velocity and Acceleration

Chapter 11 described the forces that cause objects to move. Now, let's take a look at *how* they move. To do this, we are going to need to do some measuring and some calculating to come up with mathematical quantities (amounts).

THE MATH OF MOTION

From a mathematical point of view, it's important to make a distinction between two ways of thinking about motion. There are two types of quantities: **vector** and **scalar**.

Vectors are quantities that are described by both a **magnitude** and a **direction**.

Scalars are quantities described by a **magnitude** alone.

Table 12.1 Scalar and Vector Quantities

Scalars	Vectors
Distance – how much ground an object has covered during its motion (for example, 20 meters).	**Displacement** – how far out of place an object is, or the object's change in position (for example, 20 meters east).
Speed – how fast an object is moving: distance traveled /time traveled (for example, 55 miles per hour).	**Velocity** – the rate at which an object changes its position: distance/time in a specific direction (for example, 55 miles per hour east).
	Acceleration – the rate at which an object changes its velocity. An object is accelerating if it is changing its velocity (speed or direction or both).

DISTANCE AND DISPLACEMENT

When you think of distance and displacement, you might think of a scene in a movie that is shot from two different points of view. They describe the same situation, but in two completely different ways. To demonstrate the difference, let's imagine your coach has your basketball team run court laps. On each lap, you run 84 feet east, then 50 feet south, then 84 feet west, and finally 50 feet north to end up where you started.

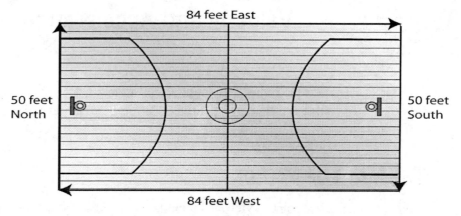

84 feet East

50 feet
North

50 feet
South

84 feet West

Figure 12.1 Your Training Exercise

When you are done with a lap, you will have run a total **distance** of 268 feet around the gym floor. However, if you look at where you went, you see that the ending point is the same as the beginning point. There was no **displacement** at all! Remember that displacement is a vector quantity, meaning you have to consider where the object moves. The movement south cancelled out the movement north, and the movement west cancelled out the movement east — so, mathematically, your displacement during this training exercise is 0 feet!

SPEED AND VELOCITY

An object's **speed** is how fast it is moving. A fast-moving object has a high speed and a slow-moving object has a low speed. An object with no movement at all has a speed of zero. We can look at an object's speed at a specific point in time (its **instantaneous speed**), or we can look at its average speed. The **average speed** can be thought of as the average of all instantaneous speeds for the trip, but when we calculate it mathematically, we use a simple ratio of distance traveled, per time of travel (for example, miles per hour or meters per second).

$$Average\ Speed = \frac{Distance\ traveled}{Time\ of\ travel}$$ **Equation 12.1**

Velocity is the rate at which an object changes its position. Velocity is a vector quantity, so you have to consider direction. We calculate the **instantaneous velocity** just like we would instantaneous speed, only we add the direction of movement.

When we calculate the **average velocity**, though, it's quite different, because we have to think about displacement instead of distance. When we calculate the average velocity of an object, we also use a ratio, but instead of distance we use displacement. It looks like this:

$$Average\ Velocity = \frac{Displacement}{Time\ of\ travel} \qquad \textbf{Equation 12.2}$$

You could have an average speed of 20 kilometers/hour for a 3-minute car trip. But if you simply drove around your neighborhood and back home, you would have a zero displacement and thus a zero average velocity.

So, the highest velocities are achieved by maximizing the amount of displacement from the original position. If you think about it, this is done by proceeding in a straight line and never changing directions.

ACCELERATION

Acceleration is another vector quantity, but it is different from velocity. Acceleration is the rate at which an object changes its velocity. To put it another way, any time the velocity of an object changes, it is accelerating. The following three things are worth noting.

- Increasing the velocity is a positive acceleration.
- Decreasing the velocity is a negative acceleration, or **deceleration**.
- Changing directions (turning) causes a decrease in velocity, and so is also a deceleration.

GRAPHING MATTERS

There are many ways to represent the motion of objects. So far you've used words, numbers and mathematical formulas to describe motion. But sometimes a scientist like you needs to see the motion of objects in a more visual way. For this, we need graphs. It is often much faster to look at the trend represented in a graph than it is to use numbers in a table or a mathematical formula. Graphs help us understand the past movements of an object or to predict future movements.

Velocity and Acceleration

Take a look at the tables and graphs to follow. What can you tell about the speed of the objects just by looking at the graphs?

Table 12.2 Displacement Over Time, Numerically

Time (seconds)	Object 1 (displacement in meters)	Object 2 (displacement in meters)
0	0	0
1	6	1
2	12	5
3	18	15
4	24	20

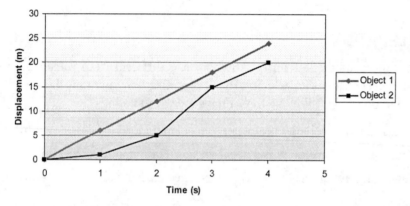

Figure 12.2 Displacement Over Time, Graphically

From looking at the two graphed lines, you can quickly tell that one of them (Object #1) is traveling at a constant speed (distance over time). Object #1 travels 6 meters for every second. This pattern results in a straight line (one which has a constant **slope**) going up and to the right. It is easy to predict the position of Object #1 at the fifth second, by noticing the pattern in the table that it moves six meters each second. It is even easier to do this by looking at the line in the graph, and simply plotting the next point on the line!

On the other hand, Object #2 is moving at changing speeds so there is no straight line. It would be harder to predict the displacement of Object #2 in the next second, because its movements have no pattern.

Now let's look at the graphs of the average velocity over each 1-second time frame for Objects #1 and #2.

Table 12.3 Velocity Over Time, Numerically

Time Frame (seconds)	Velocity of Object #1 (meters/second moving north)	Velocity of Object #2 (meters/second moving north)
0 – 1	6	1
1 – 2	6	4
2 – 3	6	10
3 – 4	6	5

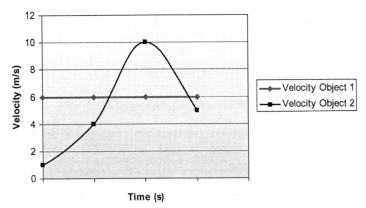

Figure 12.3 Velocity Over Time, Graphically

How does this graph compare to the position/time graph (Figure 12.2)? Well, here we have graphed the change in velocity of each object over a 1-second time frame, rather than the change in displacement measured every second.

And, just like the graph in Figure 12.2, one line represents a constant and one does not…only this time both of the graphs show acceleration, not speed. Remember, acceleration is the rate of change in velocity over time. In Figure 12.3, we can see that the velocity of Object #1 changes at 6 meters/second every second. This produces a flat line, which means *zero acceleration*! In contrast, Object #2 speeds up (accelerates) over the first three 1-second time periods. This produces a graphed line that points upward, going left to right. Then Object #2 slows down over the last 1-second time period. (Remember, when an object slows down, we call it deceleration, which is the same as *negative acceleration*.) This produces a graphed line that points downward, going left to right.

Now that you understand how these graphs work, take a look at them *without the tables* and see if you can recognize the patterns just from the way the lines are facing…then you'll REALLY be an expert!

Challenge Question

The average velocity of Object #1 during the 0 –1 second time frame was 6m/s north. Use the data in this chapter to make an inference about the instantaneous velocity of Object #1 at 0.1, 0.5 and 0.9 seconds.

CHAPTER 12 REVIEW

Juan stands at the starting line of a race track. He leaps forward as the starting gun blasts, and runs straight toward the finish line. When he crosses the finish line 2 seconds later, he is clocked at 9 meters/second.

1. What quantitative data is given in this passage?

    A. Juan's average velocity   C. Juan's displacement

    B. Juan's average speed   D. Juan's instantaneous velocity

2. Which statement correctly describes Juan's sprint?

    A. Over 2 seconds, Juan's velocity increased by 18 m/s.

    B. Over 2 seconds, Juan has traveled 18 meters.

    C. Over 2 seconds, Juan's velocity increased to 9 m/s.

    D. Over 2 seconds, Juan's acceleration increased to 9 m/s.

3. What can you infer about how fast Juan was going 1 second into the sprint?

    A. He had travelled 9 meters.   C. His acceleration was negative.

    B. His acceleration was positive.   D. His acceleration was zero.

4. What would the graph of the velocity of Juan's sprint **most likely**, look like?

    A. a flat line

    B. a line that increases from left to right

    C. a line that decreases from left to right

    D. a line that increases from right to left

5. What information do you need to determine Juan's displacement?

    A. his average velocity over the course of the 2-second sprint

    B. his instantaneous velocity at 1 second

    C. his acceleration over the 0 to1 second time frame.

    D. his average acceleration over the course of the 2-second sprint

1. Ⓐ Ⓑ Ⓒ Ⓓ
2. Ⓐ Ⓑ Ⓒ Ⓓ
3. Ⓐ Ⓑ Ⓒ Ⓓ
4. Ⓐ Ⓑ Ⓒ Ⓓ
5. Ⓐ Ⓑ Ⓒ Ⓓ

Chapter 13
Forces and Motion

What makes objects move?

What makes them STOP moving?

These same questions have been asked for a long time, even as far back as the 1600s. At that time, a scientist named Isaac Newton struggled with both the math and the philosophy required to describe motion. Over many years, and with a great deal of collaboration and debate, Newton answered your questions and many others. The answers are found in his three Laws of Motion.

Here is **Newton's First Law of Motion,** an object at rest tends to stay at rest and an object in motion tends to stay in motion with the same speed and in the same direction unless acted upon by an unbalancing force. Another way of putting it is that objects tend to keep on doing whatever they are doing, unless something makes them do something else! The tendency for objects to resist changes in movement is called **inertia**. So, sometimes this law is also called the Law of Inertia.

Figure 13.1 A Rock Experiencing Inertia

Figure 13.2 A Rock Experiencing an Unbalancing Force

A LITTLE NEWTON IN EVERYDAY LIFE

You've probably experienced many applications of Newton's First Law of Motion without even realizing it. Consider some of your experiences in a car. Have you ever had a soda while riding in the car? Have you noticed its behavior? Soda behaves badly when the car accelerates or slows down, doesn't it? If the car accelerates from a rest, as the car accelerates forward it moves out from under the soda. Unless you have a tight lid on that pesky soda, it will spill in your lap. The opposite is also true. When slowing down quickly from a state of motion, soda continues forward with the same speed and in the same direction as the car was moving in. Ultimately, it will probably hit the windshield or the dashboard. The conclusion? You got it:

Soda in motion tends to stay in motion.

Figure 13.3 Soda Behaving Badly

ALL OBJECTS MUST "USE THE FORCE"

No, this isn't a reference to the well-known "Jedi philosophy." It's an observation that all objects (even objects at rest) are "acted upon" by forces. What ARE forces anyway? A **force** is a push or pull on an object, resulting from its interaction with another object. This may not be the definition you expected, but give it some thought. Whenever there is an interaction between two objects, there is a force exerted on each of the objects. When the interaction stops, the two objects stop experiencing the influence of the forces between them. Sometimes the interaction is easy to see because it's a **direct contact force**. The interaction is more difficult to see when the influence is exerted over a distance (naturally, these are called **at-a-distance forces**).

Contact forces are types of forces where two interacting objects are in physical contact with each other. Examples of contact forces include **frictional forces**, **normal forces** and **applied forces**.

Table 13.1 Forces Described

Applied Force	a force applied to an object by a person or another object. If a person pushes a book across a desk, there is an applied force acting on the book.
Normal Force	the support force exerted upon an object in contact with another stable object. If a book is resting on a desk, then the desk is exerting a "normal" upward force on the book in order to support the weight of the book.
Frictional Force	the force exerted by a surface as an object moves across it or makes an effort to move across it. The frictional force opposes the motion of the object. If a book moves across the surface of a desk, then the desk exerts a frictional force in the opposite direction of its motion. The amount of friction depends on the nature of the two surfaces and on the degree to which they are pressed together.

Action-at-a-distance forces are types of forces where even though the two interacting objects are not in physical contact with each other, they still able to exert a push or pull. Here are some examples of action-at-a-distance forces, with a little explanation.

- **Gravitational forces**: Jumping. Your feet leave the ground and you are no longer in contact with the Earth. However, there is a gravitational pull between you and the Earth. It is the thing that pulls you back down.

- **Electrical forces**: Opposites attract. Think of the attraction between positive protons and negative electrons in atoms. They do not touch, but are nonetheless pulled toward each other.

- **Magnetic forces**: Just think about magnets. Two magnets exert a magnetic pull or push on each other even when separated by a distance of a few centimeters.

Forces are **vector** quantities. That means they are stated in terms of both magnitude (size) and direction. (It also means you have to remember to mention both of these when describing the forces acting on an object.) Force is measured in SI units of newtons.

In Table 13.1, we described contact forces in terms of the forces acting on a book which was resting on a table. If the book is not moving, we know that the downward force of gravity and the upward force of the table supporting the book (the normal force) are equal and acting in opposite directions. This state of affairs, where the forces are balanced in both direction and in magnitude, results in a stationary object.

Let's say that we want to move our resting object. To slide the book across the table, we would apply a pushing force and let go. If the book moves, we have overcome both its "at rest" inertia and any forces (like friction) that would oppose the book's motion. Before this new force is applied, the forces balance. Once the new force is applied, though, the forces become unbalanced. The result is that the book would slide in the direction of the applied force.

But would it keep on sliding forever? Doesn't the Law of Inertia say that it will?

No, actually it doesn't. The book is moving, so we know that the force applied in the direction of movement is *unbalanced* by another force. It is not, however, *unopposed* by other forces. The frictional force of the table opposes the movement of the book. Over time, the book will stop moving. Once the book stops moving, the forces are balanced once again and the book is at rest.

There is a saying that goes "a picture is worth a thousand words." This is true for forces as well. Since forces are vectors and have direction, it seems pretty logical that we represent them with arrows in vector diagrams. What is a vector diagram? **Vector diagrams** are diagrams used to show the direction and relative magnitude (size) of a vector quantity. The size of the arrow shows the magnitude of the force, and the direction of the arrow shows the direction in which the force is pushing or pulling.

Take a look at this vector diagram and see if you can figure out what it shows:

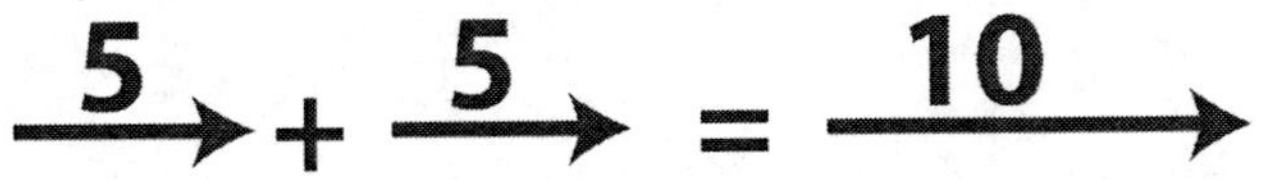

$$\underrightarrow{5} + \underrightarrow{5} = \underrightarrow{10}$$

Figure 13.4 Additive Vector Diagram

You have probably guessed that the diagram shows one force of 5 newtons (N) moving to the right, adding to another force of 5 N moving to the right. This equals a total force of 10 N moving to the right. Let's look at another.

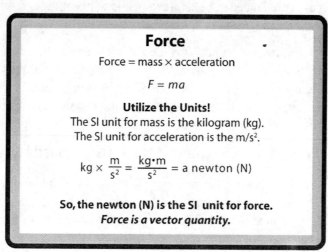

Figure 13.5 Subtractive Vector Diagram

In the diagram above, we have something very different going on. There is a force of 10 N pushing up, and a force of 5 N pushing down, creating a net force of 5 N pushing up. A **net force** is the sum of all the forces acting on an object. Remember that forces have magnitude and direction (a vector) and if two forces are equally acting in opposite directions, they will cancel each other out!

So, the effect of an unbalanced force is to move an object. Let's look at this another way, though. What amount of force is exerted by a moving object? Equation 13.1 shows us how to figure this out.

Force

Force = mass × acceleration

$$F = ma$$

Utilize the Units!
The SI unit for mass is the kilogram (kg).
The SI unit for acceleration is the m/s^2.

$$kg \times \frac{m}{s^2} = \frac{kg \cdot m}{s^2} = a \text{ newton (N)}$$

So, the newton (N) is the SI unit for force.
Force is a vector quantity.

Equation 13.1

Equation 13.1 shows us that force is related to both the mass and the acceleration of an object. So, you might infer that an object that is not accelerating and cannot exert a force. Well, yes, that would be true, except that there is nothing in the universe that is not accelerating (or decelerating). Even that book — you know, the one sitting on the table that we described in Table 13.1? That book is still (that is, it was not moving in any rate that we could observe), but it was accelerating! Let's take a closer look at gravity and see.

GRAVITATIONAL FORCE

Sir Isaac Newton also formulated the **universal law of gravity**. This law states the following:

- Every object in the universe pulls on every other object;

- The more mass an object has, the greater its gravitational force (pull);

- The greater the distance between two objects, the less attraction they have for each other.

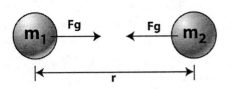

Figure 13.6 Attractive Gravitational Force Between Two Masses

Gravity gives the mass of an object its weight. Many confuse the terms "mass" and "weight." Mass is *not* the same as weight. As we know, mass measures the amount of matter an object consists of. **Weight** is a measure of the force of gravity exerted on an object by the Earth. Weight depends on the mass of the object and its distance from the Earth. In the SI measurement system, weight is measured in newtons, the same unit as force.

Gravity is a force that attracts objects to one another. In other words, it is a force that pulls. Objects are pulled or accelerate toward the Earth at a rate of about 9.81 m/s^2. This is referred to as the **free-fall acceleration**, or the acceleration due to gravity. If you drop a ball, the Earth's gravity will cause that ball to accelerate towards the Earth's surface at 9.81 meters per second, each second. This value for acceleration can be substituted into Equation 13.1 and multiplied by mass to calculate weight. Since acceleration due to gravity on the Earth is different than the gravity on the Moon, you do not weigh the same on the Earth as you would on the Moon. Your mass, however, is constant. Equation 13.2 is the formula to calculate weight. It replaces "force" with "weight," and "acceleration" with "acceleration due to gravity."

Weight

Weight = mass × acceleration due to gravity

$$W = mg$$

Utilize the Units!

g is the free fall acceleration, with units of m/s^2
The SI unit for mass is the kilogram.

$$kg \times \frac{m}{s^2} = \frac{kg \cdot m}{s^2} = N$$

So, weight is a force, and its SI unit is the newton (N).
The force of weight is a vector quantity.

Equation 13.2

Activity

Draw a vector diagram that corresponds to each of the following situations.

1. A bulldozer exerts 500 N of force on a crate to move it to the right. The crate experiences a downward gravitation force of 200 N and an upward normal force of 200 N. An opposing frictional force of 150 N is also present.

2. Marla and Johnny press their palms together and push against each other. Marla pushes Johnny with a force of 10 N. Johnny pushes Marla with a force of 12 N.

3. Marylynn stands poised at the end of a balance beam. Then she jumps off. Finally, she lands. Draw three vector diagrams, one for each stage. Which two diagrams look alike? and why?

Challenge Activity

This vector diagram corresponds to the discussion in the chapter. Use the diagram to answer the following questions.

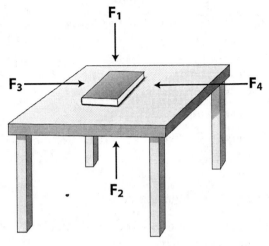

1. Define the four forces in the diagram, according to the discussion in the text.

_____

_____

2. If F_1 equals 9.81 N, what does F_2 equal?

_____

3. Describe what must happen to the forces in order for the book to move to the left.

_____

_____

_____

4. Describe what must happen to the forces in order for the book to move up.

_____

_____

_____

CHAPTER 13 REVIEW

Use the image to answer questions 1 – 4.

1. When the golf ball is at rest, what is the value of F_1?

    A. It is equal to F_2.
    B. It is equal to F_3.
    C. It is equal to F_4.
    D. It is equal to zero.

2. The golfer hits the ball with an applied force of F_3 and it launches into the sky. Which other force must have increased in value as it flies off the tee?

    A. F_1, the normal force of the tee
    B. F_2, the gravitational force
    C. F_4, the frictional force of air resistance
    D. All of these forces would have increased.

3. The golfer hits the ball with an applied force of F_3 and it launches into the sky. Which force must have disappeared as it flies off the tee?

    A. F_1, the normal force of the tee
    B. F_2, the gravitational force
    C. F_4, the frictional force of air resistance
    D. F_3, the applied force of the golf club.

4. A wind begins to blow from behind the golfer, toward the flag. Without knowing the magnitude, what could you do to correct the vector diagram in light of this new event?

    A. Write in a new arrow in the same direction as F_3.
    B. Write in a new arrow in the same direction as F_4.
    C. Write in a new arrow in the same direction as F_2.
    D. Nothing; no correction is necessary, since wind is not a force.

5. Inertia is best described as

    A. the tendency for objects to resist force.
    B. the tendency for objects to move.
    C. the tendency for objects to resist changes in motion.
    D. the tendency for objects to decelerate.

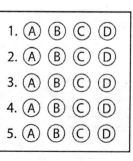

1. Ⓐ Ⓑ Ⓒ Ⓓ
2. Ⓐ Ⓑ Ⓒ Ⓓ
3. Ⓐ Ⓑ Ⓒ Ⓓ
4. Ⓐ Ⓑ Ⓒ Ⓓ
5. Ⓐ Ⓑ Ⓒ Ⓓ

Chapter 14
Work

WORKING HARD OR HARDLY WORKING

Work is a word used many ways in conversation. In science, however, it has a very specific meaning. Suppose you are investigating an exciting concept in your science class and your teacher gives you a challenging homework assignment. Later that night, you get down to work. After you complete the assignment, you announce to your parents that you are finished with your work. One of them smiles and tells you that you have done no work at all. As disappointing as that sounds, they are absolutely right! From a scientific perspective, work only happens when an applied force causes an object to move, in the direction of the force. If you think back to our discussion of vectors and scalars, you'll probably remember the term **displacement**. Work occurs when a force displaces an object in the direction of the force.

Let's take a look at another situation to clarify what is and isn't work. If your parents' car were to stall in front of your house, they might ask you to help push it into the driveway to get it off the street. You go behind the car and give it all you've got, but the car is too heavy and doesn't move. Guess what? You haven't done any work.

How can that be? If I pushed that hard, I must have done some work!

Unfortunately, no. Remember the definition: work only takes place when a force *causes motion*!

Here's another example to think about. You and your parents are late getting to the airport to catch a plane for your family vacation. You have a heavy suitcase and you are running through the airport to get to the gate on time. Although you will be very tired, when you get to the gate, you will not have done any work.

Why not? If I ran all that way, I moved the suitcase, right?

Well, yes, you moved the suitcase *horizontally*. However, the force you applied to the suitcase is a lifting force (a *vertical force*). This means the motion is happening in a different direction from the force, so no work has been done.

THE MATHEMATICS OF WORK

A weightlifter goes into a training room where there are two barbells. One is a 150-newton barbell and the other is 200 newtons. (Remember, the SI unit for force is the newton.) So, it should take 150N of vertical force to lift one of the barbells and 200 newtons to lift the other. The weightlifter lifts up one, places it down, and then lifts the other. Which lift caused the lifter to do more work? It might seem logical to say the heavier weight caused more work to be done, because more force would be needed to lift it. But from a scientific point of view, you do not have enough information to answer the question! In order to know how much work has been done, you have to know the displacement of the object. In other words, until you know how far each barbell was lifted, you really don't know how much work has been done. To figure this out mathematically, you multiply the force used (F) by the distance (d) the force caused the object to travel. It is important to remember that the distance traveled *must be* in the same direction as the force applied.

$$W = F \times d$$ **Equation 14.1**

Force is expressed in newtons, and distance in the metric system is expressed in meters, so it makes sense that one way to describe units of work would be in newton-meters. Another name for these units is the **joule (J)**. If the weightlifter in our last example lifted both barbells a distance of two meters, these would be the calculations that expressed the amount of work being done:

Table 14.1 Work Calculations

$W = F \times d$	$W = F \times d$
W = 150 N × 2 m	W = 200 N × 2 m
W = 300 J	W = 400 J

As expected, more work took place lifting the 200-newton barbell, when both barbells were lifted the same distance. So, increasing the amount of force applied increases the amount of work done. Don't forget about distance, though! As you can see from Equation 14.1, increasing the distance the object moves should also increase the work done. Perform the same calculation as in Table 14.1, but this time have the weightlifter lift the 150 N barbell 3 meters and the 200 N barbell 2 meters. The mathematical answer that you get should show you that the smaller applied force sometimes requires more work, if it is moved a greater distance.

MACHINES

You are riding home in your parents' car from an after-school event. Suddenly you hear a loud BOOM and realize that your car has blown a tire. Dad says to go to the trunk and get out the jack. You think:

Why is it easier to lift a car with a jack than with your bare hands?

Well, OK…you probably didn't think that, because you intuitively knew that the car was too heavy to lift. You need a machine to help. A **machine** is something that makes work easier by changing the size or direction of a force. A **simple machine** is any device that only requires the application of a *single* force to work. They are called "simple" because most of them don't have any moving parts! These are shown in Figure 14.1.

When you combine more than one simple machine, you have a **complex machine** (can openers, scissors, a doorknob, a car jack).

So, do simple machines reduce the amount of work?

Actually, no. A simple machine reduces the amount of effort (force) needed to move something, so the work *seems* easier. Let's look at four of the simplest simple machines.

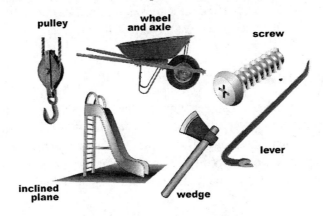

Figure 14.1 Simple Machines

Inclined planes are also called ramps. Ramps help us move things to a higher elevation with less effort. There is a trade-off, though, and that is we have to move them farther. Think about it this way: if you wanted to put a heavy box on the roof of your school, you could use a ladder (and expend a lot of force/effort climbing each step) or you could use a ramp. To reach the roof of your school, though, you'd need a pretty long ramp! Using a ramp decreases the force that you must apply, but increases the distance that you have to move the object.

A **wedge** is a double inclined plane. However, wedges have a different purpose than the inclined plane. Instead of helping you move things to higher elevations, wedges help you push things apart. The blade of an axe or knife is a wedge. How do they make work seem easier? The narrower the wedge (or the sharper the blade end of a wedge), the easier it is drive it into something and push things apart.

Screws are usually used to hold things together, like pieces of wood, metal or concrete. You may not have thought of this before, but a screw is really an *inclined plane* wrapped around a cylinder, with a *wedge* at the sharp, pointed end. The inclined plane going up the cylinder of a screw is called the threading. Turning the screw allows the threading to bite into the surrounding material, and forces the wedge tip through the material. The wider the threads of a screw, the harder it is to turn. Narrower threads make the screw easier to turn, but there are more of them. This means you will have to turn the screw more times to force the wedge tip completely into the object you are trying to put together.

Our next simple machine is the **lever**. When you think about it, just about everything that has a handle attached to it has a lever. When you first look at a lever, all you probably see is a stick. Now…think like the scientist you are and expand that idea. Two things must be considered when using a lever — the length of the "stick" and the place where it pivots. The point on which the lever pivots is called the **fulcrum**. A crowbar pivots on the very end, but a see-saw usually pivots in the middle. By changing where you put the

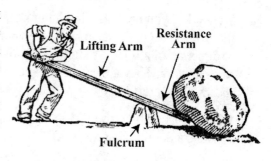

Figure 14.2 The Lever

fulcrum, you make it easier or harder to lift a heavy load. The closer to the load you put the fulcrum, the easier the load is to lift. Where's the trade-off? Lengthening the lifting arm without moving the fulcrum (that is, getting a longer stick) also makes the load easier to lift, the longer the lifting arm becomes, the greater the distance you must move it to lift the object.

ADVANTAGE – MACHINES

By now you have realized that not all machines are the same. Some machines make it easier to do work than others — they offer a greater advantage. This advantage is called **mechanical advantage**. How do we measure mechanical advantage? If you think of a machine as having an **input force** (the force you put into it) and an **output force** (the force the machine applies to move an object) then the mechanical advantage of the machine (mathematically) is the output force divided by the input force.

$$MA = \frac{\textbf{Output Force}}{\textbf{Input Force}}$$ **Equation 14.3**

Let's look at a practical example. If you put 10 newtons of force into your machine and it applies 40 newtons to move your object, then the mechanical advantage would be 40/10, or 4. Basically, that means that the machine makes it 4 times easier for you to do the work. Pretty nifty.

You might know how helpful the machine is by doing the above calculation, but how do you know how **efficient** the machine is in translating the work we put into it into the work it does for us? To put it another way, how do you know how much force is lost (used up) by the machine (through friction, for example)? To find the **mechanical efficiency** of a machine, divide the amount of work output (work the machine does for you) by the amount of work input (work you put into the machine). Then, multiply that amount by 100 to get a percentage.

$$ME = \frac{\textbf{Work Output}}{\textbf{Work Input}} \times 100$$ **Equation 14.4**

It's important to remember that no machine is 100% efficient, because all machines have some point of friction. **Friction** is a result of the interaction of material of the machine with the objects that it operates on.

> **Example:** The wheels of a wheelbarrow experience friction as they roll up a concrete ramp.

Example: The metal of a screw experiences friction as it is drilled through a block of wood.

Friction eats away at work output by resisting movement. The important thing is to know where these points of friction are and to devise ways to reduce them. Why? When you reduce the friction in the machine, work output increases and work input decreases. So efficiency goes up!

MA Example: The Inclined Plane

The mechanical advantage of the ramp comes from the ratio of the length of the ramp (L) to the height of the ramp (h), as in:

$$\frac{L}{h} = \frac{F_r}{F_e} \qquad \textbf{Equation 14.5}$$

Here we have used F_r for the output force of the machine, and F_e for the input force that you apply. Think of F_e as your effort force.

To illustrate, let's look at two scenarios that confront Pete, who wants to lift a 100N box a vertical distance of 1 meter into the back of a moving van.

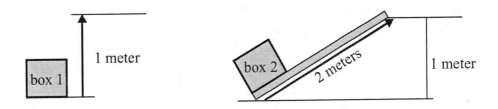

Figure 14.3 Mechanical Advantage of the Inclined Plane

In scenario A, Pete lifts the box straight up. The work that he does is:

$$W = F \times d = 100N \times 1m = 100 \text{ J}$$

In scenario B, Pete chooses to push the box up a 2 meter ramp to get it into the van. The work that he does is the same, 100J. The reason is that the weight is distributed by the angle of the ramp. Pete actually only has to push part of the weight of the box up the ramp. Let's find out how much MA he has gained by using the ramp instead of a straight lift.

From Equation 14.5, you can see that the mechanical advantage of the inclined plane equals the length of the plane divided by the height of the plane's terminal end. (the end that is lifted up). In our example this is:

$$\text{MA} = \frac{L}{h} = \frac{2 \text{ meters}}{1 \text{ meter}} = 2$$

That means that Pete's effort force, when using the plane, is

$$F_e = \frac{F_r}{\text{MA}} = \frac{100 \text{ N}}{2} = 50 \text{ N}$$

So, using the inclined plane made the work *easier.* You know it was easier, because it required a lower effort force to move the box up the ramp than it did to lift it straight up.

In real life, an inclined plane will have friction that opposes motion (that is, it makes things harder to move). Remember, friction decreases mechanical advantage. What would be the mechanical advantage of the inclined plane if Pete had to apply an additional 10 N of force to overcome friction as he pushed the box up the inclined plane?

$$\text{MA} = \frac{F_r}{F_e} = \frac{100\text{ N}}{50\text{ N} + 10\text{ N}} = \frac{100\text{ N}}{60\text{ N}} = 1\frac{2}{3}$$

The force necessary to move the box up the inclined plane is still less than lifting it vertically, but friction increases the effort force and, therefore, decreases the mechanical advantage.

*Test tip: The mechanical advantage of a frictionless inclined plane will always be the length of the plane (in our example, 2 meters) divided by the height of the plane's terminal end (in our example, 1 meter).

MA Example: The Lever

Another simple machine is the lever. The important parts of a lever are the **fulcrum**, which supports and distributes weight, the resistance arm and the effort arm. The mechanical advantage of a lever comes from manipulating the length of the arms: L_e is the length of the effort arm and L_r is the length of the resistance arm. The equation is:

$$\frac{L_e}{L_r} = \frac{F_r}{F_e}$$

A seesaw is a perfect example of a lever. On a seesaw, the fulcrum is placed in the center, between two equal length arms…which means that its mechanical advantage is one, right? Well, yes, because a seesaw is made for fun, not work.

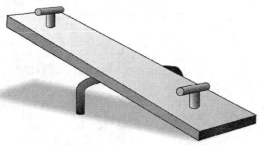

Figure 14.4 The Simplest Lever

So think about a modified seesaw, where one side (L_e) is 2 meters and the other (L_r) is 0.5 meters. The mechanical advantage of this lever is

$$\text{MA} = \frac{L_e}{L_r} = \frac{2\text{ meters}}{0.5\text{ meters}} = 4$$

Now, if Wanda puts her 6N bookbag at the end of the resistance arm (that is the short arm), what kind of effort force must be used to lift it 3 meters? That is:

$$F_e = \frac{F_r}{MA} = \frac{6\,N}{4} = 1.5\,N$$

So, Wanda needs to apply 6 N of effort force to lift the bookbag by herself, but only 1.5 N of effort force to lift it using the lever. Now *that* is a mechanical advantage!

MA Example: The Pulley

In the simplest arrangement, a pulley is fixed and immovable (Figure 14.5). In this arrangement, a 100 N load will require a 100 N of effort, that is, the mechanical advantage is 1 (100 N/100 N).

$$MA = \frac{F_r}{F_e}$$
$$= \frac{100\,N}{100\,N} = 1$$

Although this does not reduce the effort required to lift heavy loads, it does allow you to change the direction that you must lift.

A moveable pulley is more versatile. This type of pulley hangs from a rope attached at one end. The effort force is split, as shown in Figure 14.6.

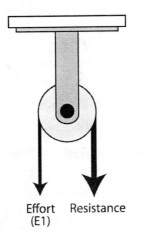

Effort   Resistance
(E1)

Figure 14.5 The Fixed Pulley

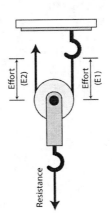

Figure 14.6 A Movable Pulley

A moveable pulley has a greater mechanical advantage than a fixed pulley because both sides of the rope exert an equal effort force on the load. That means that the man pulling on one side of the rope is only exerting half of the effort force.

$$MA = \frac{F_r}{F_e}$$
$$= \frac{100\,N}{50\,N} = 1$$

More complex pulley systems can be designed by attaching more pulleys to one another.

CHAPTER 14 REVIEW

1. Which of the following scenarios results in work being done?

   A. hammering a nail into a board
   C. pulling on a 1000 N boulder
   B. pushing on a concrete wall
   D. playing air guitar

2. An 10N box must be moved onto a closet shelf 2.5 meters above Darell's head. How long should an inclined plane be to have a mechanical advantage of 2?

   A. 25 m
   B. 1.25 m
   C. 5 m
   D. 10 m

3. Increasing the length of the lifting arm of a lever without moving the fulcrum will

   A. make the load easier to lift.
   B. make the load harder to lift.
   C. increase the horizontal distance that you can move the lifting arm.
   D. decrease the vertical distance that you can move the lifting arm.

4. Jackson throws a ball, which arcs up, then falls down. It then bounces on the floor and springs back up. How is the work that is done calculated?

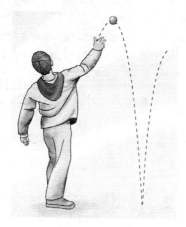

   A. using the distance the ball travels from where the ball leaves Jackson's hand, to where it begins to fall toward the floor
   B. using the distance the ball travelled in Jackson's hand as he throws the ball
   C. using the distance the ball travels from where the ball leaves Jackson's hand, to where it hits the floor
   D. using the distance between Jackson's hand and where the ball finally comes to rest

5. What is one way to increase efficiency?

   A. increase friction
   B. decrease friction
   C. increase work input
   D. decrease work output

1. Ⓐ Ⓑ Ⓒ Ⓓ
2. Ⓐ Ⓑ Ⓒ Ⓓ
3. Ⓐ Ⓑ Ⓒ Ⓓ
4. Ⓐ Ⓑ Ⓒ Ⓓ
5. Ⓐ Ⓑ Ⓒ Ⓓ

Chapter 15
Electromagnetic Force

ELECTROMAGNETIC FORCE

The electromagnetic force should also be quite familiar to you, although you might think of it more naturally in terms of its component forces, the electrical force and the magnetic force. The **electrical force** causes static electricity and drives the flow of electric charge (electric current) in electrical conductors. The **magnetic force** is associated with magnets. These two forces are caused by their respective fields — in effect, the field produces the force.

The electric and magnetic fields are interconnected. For example, the presence of an electric field will actually produce a magnetic field. Similarly, a change in the magnetic field produces an electric field. Because the fields are so intimately linked, they are referred to simply as the electromagnetic field. The **electromagnetic force** is the force exerted by the electromagnetic field on any charged particle.

The electromagnetic force is different from the gravitational force, though both are fundamental forces. The gravitational force describes the push and pull of the components of the universe, based on *mass and distance*. The electromagnetic force describes the push and pull of the components of the universe, based on *charge and distance*.

The electromagnetic force is powerful down to a very tiny scale — it is the primary cause for the bonding between molecules and atoms.

ELECTRIC FORCE AND FIELD

The **electric force** between two charged particles is described by **Coulomb's law**. The important features of Coulomb's law are:

- Charged particles exert forces on each other.
- Like charges attract, opposite charges repel.
- The greater the distance between charges, the less force they will exert on each other.

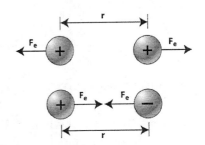

Figure 15.1 Electric Force Between Two Charged Particles

Recall that atoms are made of a positively charged nucleus surrounded by negatively charged electrons. The attractive electrical force between these charges is what holds the atom together.

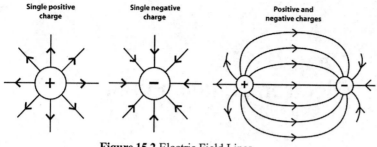

Figure 15.2 Electric Field Lines

The concept of an **electric field** helps to visualize the effects electric charges have on one another. An electric field surrounds every electric charge. If a test charge (a small, charged particle) were placed in the electric field of a charged particle, a force would be exerted upon it. The **electric field lines** or **lines of force** point in the direction that a positive charge would move when in the presence of an electric field. A positively charged particle would be repelled by a positive charge and attracted by a negative charge. Thus, electric field lines always point away from positive source charges and toward negative source charges. Electric field lines do not actually exist in the physical world; they are simply used to illustrate the direction of the electric force exerted on charged particles. The strength of the field surrounding a charged particle is dependent on how charged the particle generating the field is and separation distance between the charged objects.

MAGNETIC FORCE AND FIELD

The like poles on two magnets exhibit a repulsive (magnetic) force, but two unlike poles exhibit an attractive force. For example, the north pole of one magnet will repel the north pole of another magnet, but the north pole of one magnet will attract the south pole of another magnet.

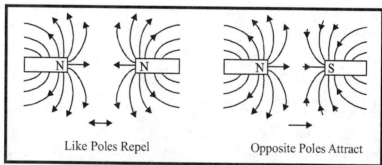

Like Poles Repel   Opposite Poles Attract

Figure 15.3 Interaction of North and South Poles

This creates a **magnetic field,** consisting of invisible lines of force around the magnet between the two poles. These invisible lines, called **magnetic field lines**, always point from the north pole to the south pole of a magnet. The Earth itself acts as a giant magnet having a North Pole and a South Pole, and the magnetic field circles the Earth longitudinally.

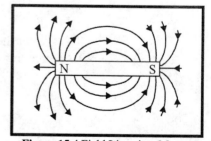

Figure 15.4 Field Lines in a Magnet

ELECTROMAGNETIC FORCE AND FIELDS

An electric current, as described in a previous section, can produce a magnetic field, and thus, a magnetic force. We know from Newton's third law that for every action there is an equal and opposite reaction. Therefore, it stands to reason that a magnet must exert a force on a wire carrying an electric current. As you can tell from this phenomenon, the electric and magnetic forces are intimately related. They are actually considered to be one force, called the **electromagnetic force**, which is one of the four fundamental forces of nature.

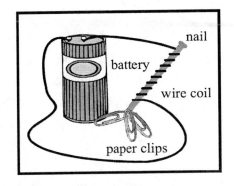

Figure 15.5 Electromagnet

Electrical and magnetic fields are related. For example, a magnetic field can be created by winding a wire around a conducting core and passing electricity through the wire. This type of man-made magnet is called an **electromagnet**. The magnetic field of an electromagnet can be strengthened by the number of turns in the wire coil or by the amount of electric current going through the wire. More coils, more current or greater voltage equates to larger magnetic force. Note that the current used to create an electromagnet is **direct current** or **DC**, which is the kind of current produced by a battery. Direct current flows in only one direction.

When an electromagnet is placed between the poles of a permanent magnet, the poles attract and repel each other as the electromagnet spins. Electrical energy is converted to mechanical energy. Electromagnets become more powerful as the amount of applied current to them is increased. They are often used to lift heavy metal objects, carry them and set them down again by turning off the current.

Not only can an electrical current create a magnetic field, but a magnet can produce an electric current by moving the magnet through a coil. Creating an electric current using a magnet is called **electromagnetic induction**. **Electric generators** are devices that use electromagnetic induction to create electricity. Figure 15.6 is a simple diagram of electromagnetic induction. Note that the magnet or the coils must be in motion in order for an electric current to be generated. The direction that the electrons travel depends on the direction that the magnet travels.

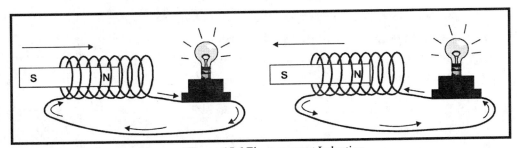

Figure 15.6 Electromagnet Induction

In the United States, electric power generators produce electricity by turning a coil between the north and south poles of a magnet. Each time the coil switches from north pole to south pole, the direction of the current changes direction. This type of current is called **alternating current** or **AC**.

CHAPTER 15 REVIEW

1. Which of the following statements is *not* true?

   A. A magnet can produce an electric field.
   B. The flow of electricity can produce a magnetic field.
   C. An electromagnet can be strengthened by increasing the number of wire coils.
   D. An electromagnet can be strengthened by decreasing the number of wire coils.

2. Jason places a bar magnet on a flat surface and covers it with a sheet of paper. Then he evenly sprinkles a layer of iron filings on top of the paper. Which of the following diagrams indicates the most likely arrangement of the filings on the paper?

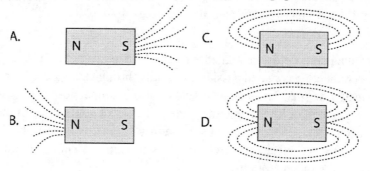

Look at the diagram below, and then answer the following question.

3. What would happen if the poles of the magnet were reversed?

   A. The direction of the current would be reversed.
   B. The light bulb would not light.
   C. No current would be produced.
   D. The current would increase.

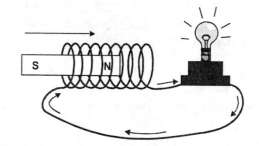

4. Which of the following will attract one another?

   A. the north pole of a magnet and the south pole of another magnet
   B. the north pole of a magnet and the north pole of another magnet
   C. the south pole of a magnet and the south pole of another magnet
   D. all of the above

5. What type of current is a wristwatch powered by?

   A. alternating
   B. direct
   C. inductive
   D. magnetic

1. Ⓐ Ⓑ Ⓒ Ⓓ
2. Ⓐ Ⓑ Ⓒ Ⓓ
3. Ⓐ Ⓑ Ⓒ Ⓓ
4. Ⓐ Ⓑ Ⓒ Ⓓ
5. Ⓐ Ⓑ Ⓒ Ⓓ

Chapter 16
Electrical Circuits

ELECTRICITY

In modern times, electrical charges and force surround us almost everywhere we go, though we don't typically think about it. Think of how dependent we are on artificial light, let alone television, computers and cell phones. All of these operate because electrical charges are in motion. A general term that describes the motion of charged particles and the energy derived from that motion is **electricity**. **Electrical current** specifically refers to the flow of electrons through a material.

For electrons to flow through a material, it must have a structure that allows for the free movement of charge. This type of material is called a **conductor**. Metals are usually good conductors. For instance, copper is a metal used to conduct electrons from one place to another. Copper is often used as electrical wire and in electrical

Figure 16.1 Copper Electrical Wire

circuits. Materials that do not allow electrons to move freely through them are called **insulators**. If you have ever seen electrical wires, you'll notice that there is a layer of plastic that surrounds the copper wire inside. The plastic acts as an insulator, retaining charge inside the wire casing and helping to safely channel it to the end application.

CURRENT ELECTRICITY

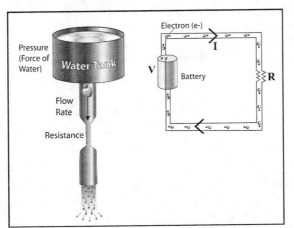

Figure 16.2 Analogy Between Flowing Water and Electric Current

To understand **electrical current**, let's compare electricity to the water flowing through a pipe. The flow rate of water in a pipe might be given in units of gallons per minute. In a similar way, electrons flow through a wire in the circuit like water flows through a pipe. **Current (I)** is the flow rate of electrons through a wire in the circuit and is measured in **amperes**. As water flowing through a pipe rubs against the walls of the pipe, the water slows down. In the same way, electrons slow down as they move through a circuit. This slowing down of the electrons is called resistance. **Electrical resistance (R)** is the measure of how difficult it is to move electrons through a circuit.

Why does water flow through a pipe? A force like gravity or the force of a pump causes water to flow. So, what force causes electrons to flow? **Voltage (V)** is the measure of the electromotive force or pressure that causes electrons to move. Voltage is measured in **volts**. One way to think of voltage is a measure of the difference in the electrical potential energy between two points. This is why voltage is synonymous with **electrical potential**. Just as a rock on top of a hill has a potential energy difference between the hilltop and the base of the hill, a typical AA battery creates 1.5 volts of electrical potential energy between the positive and negative terminals. A standard car battery is 12 volts. When the switch on an electronic device or in a car is turned on, the electrical potential energy or voltage is converted into electrical kinetic energy, that is, electrical current.

OHM'S LAW

Ohm's Law (V=IR) states that the resistance is equal to the voltage divided by the current.

Equation 16.1
Ohm's Law

Voltage = Current × Resistance

$$V = IR$$

Utilize the Units!

The SI unit for voltage is the volt (V).

$$1 \text{ volt} = \frac{1 \text{ joule}}{1 \text{ coulomb}}$$

The SI unit for current is the ampere (A).

$$1 \text{ ampere} = \frac{1 \text{ coulomb}}{\text{second}}$$

The SI unit for resistance is the ohm (Ω).

$$1 \text{ ohm } \Omega = \frac{1 \text{ volt}}{\text{amp}}$$

The volt was named for Italian physicist Alessandro Volta, who invented the voltaic pile (the first chemical battery). The ampere is named in honor of the French physicist André-Marie Ampère for his contributions to the discovery of electromagnetism. The ohm is named in honor of German physicist George Ohm, who established the fundamental relationship between voltage, current and resistance that today we call Ohm's Law.

Equation 16.1

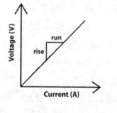

$$\frac{\text{rise}}{\text{run}} = \frac{\text{voltage}}{\text{current}} = \text{resistance}$$

Figure 16.3 Current - Voltage Relationship

You may notice that Ohm's law reveals a linear relationship between voltage and current. Given a linear graph of voltage versus current, the slope of the line (i.e. rise over run) is equal to the resistance. Thus, the resistance of a device can be determined experimentally by taking several voltage and current measurements, then plotting the data on a graph. Not all electronic devices have this linear relationship between voltage and current. Those that do have a linear relationship (that is, their output looks like Figure 16.3) are called **ohmic devices**.

Ohm's law can be used to calculate resistance, voltage or current when two of the three quantities are known.

Example: A flashlight bulb with an operating resistance of 50 ohms is connected to a 9.0 V battery. What is the current through the light bulb?

Step 1. Set up the equation: $V = I \cdot R$

Step 2. Insert the known information: $9.0 \text{ V} = I \cdot 50 \ \Omega$

Step 3. Solve: $I = \dfrac{9.0 \text{ V}}{50 \ \Omega} = 0.18 \text{ A}$

ELECTRICAL CIRCUITS

The movement of electrons is called electric current. The energy it produces is called electricity. The path through which the electricity is conducted is called a **circuit**. When we draw electrical circuits, we use the symbols shown in Figure 16.4 to represent voltage sources, resistors and wires. **Batteries** are commonly used as voltage sources. Devices such as radios and televisions draw current from the circuit, and so provide resistance to the flow of electricity. These devices, or **loads**, are usually represented as a simple resistor in circuit diagrams. There are two types of circuits: series and parallel circuits.

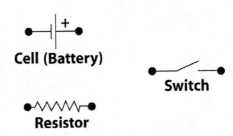

Figure 16.4 Symbols for Circuit Elements

SERIES CIRCUITS

In a **series circuit**, all current is the same through each part or load. If a resistor is broken or damaged, current will no longer be able to flow through a series circuit. Figure 16.5 shows a series circuit and Figure 16.6 shows its equivalent circuit diagram.

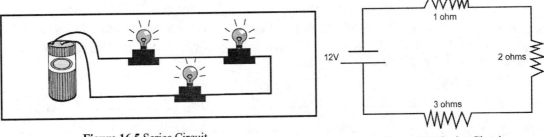

Figure 16.5 Series Circuit

Figure 16.6 Series Circuit

The three resistors represent the resistance to electrical flow provided by each light bulb. In a series circuit, you can determine the total equivalent resistance of the circuit by adding the individual resistance values. Equation 16.2 illustrates this relationship.

$$R_{eq} = R_1 + R_2 + R_3 \qquad \textbf{Equation 16.2}$$

Thus, adding a resistor in series increases the overall resistance of the circuit. All resistors in a series have the same amount of current, or amperage.

A **switch** may be used to open and close the circuit. When the switch is open, electricity will not flow.

Challenge Question 1

Determine the equivalent resistance of the circuit shown in Figure 16.6.

Just as the loads in a circuit can be connected in series, multiple batteries can be connected in series. This is done by connecting the positive end of one terminal with the negative terminal of another battery. This is shown in Figure 16.7.

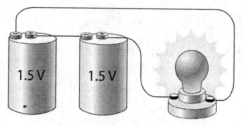

Figure 16.7 Batteries in Series

In this case, the voltage of the circuit is increased. To find the voltage of a circuit in series, add the voltages of the individual batteries together. For the circuit in Figure 16.7, you get:

$$V_{eq} = V_1 + V_2 \quad \textbf{Equation 16.3}$$

Challenge Question 2

What is the total potential of the circuit in Figure 16.7?

PARALLEL CIRCUITS

A **parallel circuit** has more than one path for the electricity to flow. The voltage is the same through all of the resistors in the circuit. If one path is removed or broken, current will still be able to flow in a parallel circuit. Most households are wired with parallel circuits, so that when you turn off a light, the television doesn't turn off as well.

Figure 16.8 Parallel Circuit

The overall resistance of a parallel circuit is reduced as more resistors are added. Thus, more current flows through the circuit. The equivalent resistance of a parallel circuit is expressed by Equation 16.4.

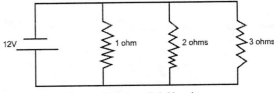

Figure 16.9 Parallel Circuit

$$\frac{1}{R_{eq}} = \frac{1}{R_1} + \frac{1}{R_2} + \frac{1}{R_3} \qquad \textbf{Equation 16.4}$$

The batteries of a circuit may also be connected in parallel. This is done by connecting the positive terminal of one battery to the positive terminal of the next battery. A parallel connection is shown in Figure 16.10.

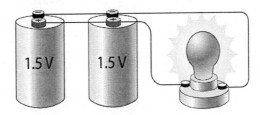

Figure 16.10 Batteries in Parallel

Connecting batteries in parallel does not increase the voltage of the circuit. The voltage of two batteries connected in parallel will equal the voltage of the lowest-voltage battery.

$$V_{eq} = V_1 = V_2 \quad \textbf{Equation 16.5}$$

Challenge Question 3

Most batteries that you encounter are 1.5 V. What is the equivalent voltage for the circuit shown in Figure 16.10?

Even though the voltage of the circuit is not increased by connecting batteries in parallel, the *capacity* of the circuit is increased. This means that the circuit has more charge to draw from, and the loads connected to it will last longer.

COMPARISON OF SERIES AND PARALLEL CIRCUITS

Let's say that you have a single 1.5 V battery as the voltage source for a circuit. You connect one load, a light bulb, to the circuit, and the light bulb lights up. Now add a second light bulb to the circuit in series. Both light bulbs will still light, but they will be dimmer than the single light bulb. You can continue to connect light bulbs to the circuit, and eventually there will not be enough electrical force (voltage) to light them all. This is shown in Figure 16.11.

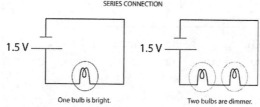

Figure 16.11 Effect of Adding Load on a Series Circuit

Note that the light bulb is drawn as a loop; this is only to distinguish the light bulb that we are talking about from other loads. Remember that a light bulb is still a resistor, a device that offers resistance to current flow in the circuit.

The situation is different if you connect your second bulb in parallel. Now both bulbs will burn equally brightly, because there is less overall resistance when two loads are connected than when one is connected.

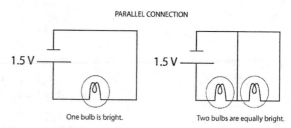

Figure 16.12 Effect of Adding a Load on a Parallel Circuit

Practice Exercise: Series and Parallel Circuits

Draw the appropriate circuit diagram based on the descriptions given. Determine the equivalent resistance (R_{eq}) in each circuit. For #1 and #2, determine the current (I) running through the circuit also.

1. Two light bulbs, one with a resistance of 100 ohms and one with a resistance of 150 ohms, are connected in series to a 25-V battery.

2. Three resistors, all with a resistance of 50 ohms, are connected in parallel to a 9-V battery.

3. A strand of lights with five bulbs are connected to a 120-V voltage source. When one bulb goes out, the other four bulbs go out as well.

4. A strand of lights with four bulbs are connected to a 210-V voltage source. When one bulb goes out, the remaining bulbs stay lit.

Challenge Activity

Identify whether these are series or parallel circuits.

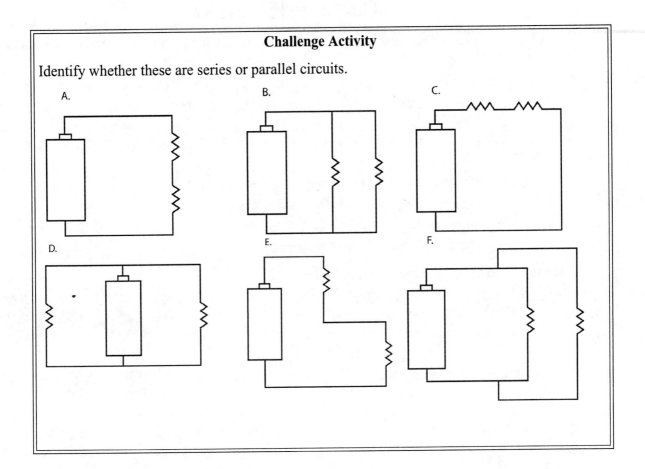

A.

B.

C.

D.

E.

F.

Challenge Activity

Use Ohm's law to draw a graph of the approximate output of a non-ohmic device. Here circuit resistance will change as voltage is applied. Make your x axis (horizontal) applied voltage (V) and your y axis (vertical) output current (I). What is the slope of your line? How does your graph look if resistance (R) increases as more voltage is applied?

CHAPTER 16 REVIEW

1. A switch is inserted into a series circuit of Christmas lights. During the night, the switch is left open. The lights will

   A. continue to burn.   C. become a parallel circuit.
   B. be turned off.   D. burn brighter.

2. A series and a parallel circuit each have two resistors of 2Ω each. A third 2Ω resistor is then added. What happens?

   A. The equivalent resistance of the parallel circuit increases.
   B. The equivalent resistance of the series circuit increases.
   C. The voltage of the series circuit decreases.
   D. The voltage of the series circuit increases.

Use the following figure to answer question 3.

3. The batteries in this flashlight

   A. are connected in series.
   B. have a resistance equal to $3\ \Omega$.
   C. are connected in parallel.
   D. have a voltage equal to 1.5V.

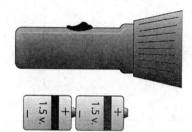

4. Renee has built a circuit with a single 1.5 V battery connected in series to three light bulbs. The light bulbs are not as bright as she would like. What can she do to make them burn more brightly?

   A. add a fourth light bulb in series   C. connect a second battery in series
   B. connect a second battery in parallel   D. A and C only

5. The flow of electricity through a circuit can be compared to the flow of water through a pipe. Using this comparison, the friction caused by the pipe wall would be similar to

   A. the resistance in the circuit.   C. the voltage of the circuit.
   B. the amperage of the circuit.   D. the coulombs in the circuit.

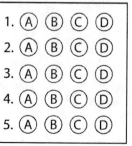

1. Ⓐ Ⓑ Ⓒ Ⓓ
2. Ⓐ Ⓑ Ⓒ Ⓓ
3. Ⓐ Ⓑ Ⓒ Ⓓ
4. Ⓐ Ⓑ Ⓒ Ⓓ
5. Ⓐ Ⓑ Ⓒ Ⓓ

Chapter 17
Electricity in Our Lives

WHERE DOES ELECTRICITY COME FROM?

As you know from learning about the Law of Conservation of Energy, energy is not made or created. The word that we use to describe where electrical energy comes from is **generated**. Electrical energy is generated by a generator.

A generator is a machine that converts mechanical energy into electrical energy. The process is based on the relationship between magnetism and electricity, which we first discussed in Chapter 15. You might remember that an electromagnetic wave has two parts: the electric part and the magnetic part. Well, it turns out that when a magnet is moved near a coil of wire, electrons are drawn from the magnet into the wire. The movement of electrons through the wire is electricity.

The generator has a series of insulated coils of wire that form a cylinder. Inside the cylinder is a rotating (turning) shaft. When the shaft rotates (turns), the magnet is moved in and out of the coils. Electrons are stripped away from the magnet and into the wire coil. The wire coil serves as an electric conductor. A conductor is a material that will allow electrons to pass through. The **rate** at which the electrons pass through the conductor is called the current. The electrons move through the wire, forming a current. The bigger the generator, the greater the current. This is the electrical power that eventually comes to your house.

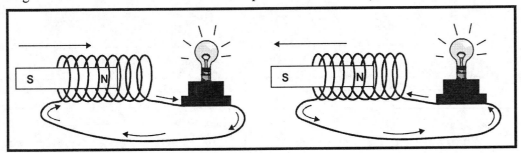

Figure 17.1 Generator

TURBINES

So, what turns the rotating shaft? A mechanical force, often water or air, is used to turn the shaft. A **turbine** converts the kinetic energy of a moving fluid (liquid or gas) into the mechanical energy that moves the magnets in the generator to make electricity. Turbines have a series of blades mounted on the shaft. The fluid is forced past the curved blades, causing them to turn the rotating shaft that is connected to the generator. When water is used to turn the turbine, it is called **hydroelectric power**. When air is used, it is called **wind power**.

USING WATER AND WIND TO TURN TURBINES

Hydroelectric power is a process in which flowing water is used to spin a turbine connected to a generator. Flowing water accumulates in reservoirs created by the use of dams. The water pushes past the turbine blades, driving the generator to produce electricity. The force of a river current can be used in place of dammed water to apply pressure to the turbine blades.

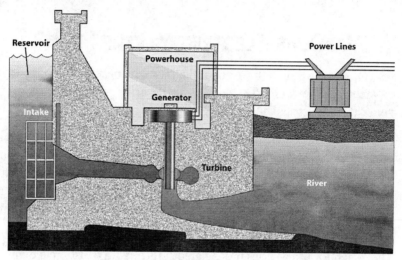

Figure 17.2 Hydroelectric Power Plant

Challenge Question

What type of energy is represented by the flowing river current, and what type is represented by dammed water? Use Figure 17.2 to describe the water that pushes the turbine.

_____

_____

Wind power is the conversion of wind energy into electricity. A wind turbine is similar to a typical windmill. It has rotating blades on the top of a wind tower. The blades turn when the wind blows, collecting the wind's kinetic energy. This drives the generator to produce electricity. This type of power production works best where there is a steady wind. Large **wind farms** are found in the plains areas of the U.S.

Figure 17.3 Wind Farm

USING STEAM TO TURN TURBINES

There are several types of power that use steam as the force that turns the turbine. In fact, in the United States, most electricity is produced in steam turbines. You might now be asking yourself

Where does the steam come from?

Steam is heated water. Energy must be used in order to create heat. That energy may be chemical (fossil fuel or biomass burning) or nuclear (nuclear fission). Natural steam may also be harnessed directly from the Earth, as in geothermal power.

Coal, petroleum (oil) and natural gas are called **fossil fuels**. These materials are burned in large furnaces to heat water and make steam. That steam then pushes on the blades of a turbine. At this time, coal is the largest source of energy used to generate electricity in the United States. Natural gas can be burned to heat water for steam, but it can also be burned to produce hot combustion gases that pass directly through a turbine. Gas turbines are often used when electricity utility usage is in high demand.

Biomass energy is the energy from plants and plant-derived materials. It has been used as far back as the first time people began burning wood to cook food and keep warm. Wood is still the largest biomass energy resource today, but other sources of biomass can also be used. These include food crops, grassy and woody plants, manure from agriculture or forestry and the decaying parts of municipal and industrial wastes. Even the fumes from landfills (which are methane, a natural gas) can be used as a biomass energy source. Biomass materials are burned in large furnaces, the same way that fossil fuels are.

Nuclear power produces steam in a different way. A nuclear power plant contains a core of nuclear fuel (usually uranium). When atoms of uranium fuel are hit by neutrons, they fission (split), releasing heat and more neutrons. These neutrons then strike more uranium atoms, splitting them, and so on. This **chain reaction** releases a great deal of heat that is then used to create steam.

Figure 17.4 Cooling Tower at a Nuclear Power Plant

Geothermal power comes from heat buried beneath the surface of the Earth. In some areas, the heat rises close to the surface of the Earth. At these "hot spots," magma from under the Earth's surface creeps through. When a power plant is built near a hot spot, energy can be generated from steam.

Figure 17.5 Geothermal Power

ELECTRICITY WITH NO TURBINES

There is another way to produce energy, one that requires no moving parts. **Solar power** comes directly from the Sun. Electricity is generated by a **photovoltaic (solar) cell**. The cell is made of a conducting material, like silicon. When the electromagnetic radiation from the Sun hits the solar cell, it causes electrons in the material to move. The movement of electrons is the electric current. Solar cells are used to power satellites, charge batteries and provide electrical power to homes.

Figure 17.6 Solar Panels

MOVING ELECTRICITY FROM PLACE TO PLACE: THE TRANSFORMER

How does electricity get from the generator into your home? It travels along transmission lines to a transformer. The **transformer** changes (transforms) electricity from low voltage to high voltage. This is an advantage because electricity can be moved long distances more efficiently using high voltage. Transmission lines are then used to carry the high-voltage electricity to a substation. There, transformers are again used to change the high-voltage electricity back into the lower-voltage electricity required in your home. From the substation, distribution lines carry the electricity to homes, offices and factories.

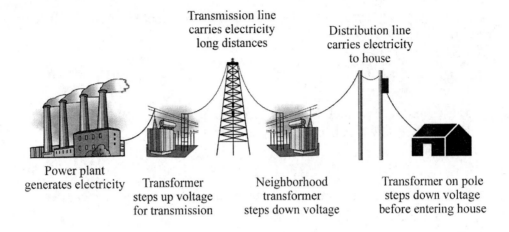

Transmission line carries electricity long distances

Distribution line carries electricity to house

Power plant generates electricity

Transformer steps up voltage for transmission

Neighborhood transformer steps down voltage

Transformer on pole steps down voltage before entering house

Figure 17.7 Transporting Electricity

ENERGY TRANSFORMATION

Now that we have examined each of these energy sources, let's summarize the energy transformations that must occur in order to generate electricity.

Table 17.1 Transformation of Energy Sources

Energy Type	Energy transformation
Chemical	Potential, chemical energy to mechanical energy to electrical energy
Nuclear	Potential, nuclear energy to heat energy to mechanical energy to electrical energy
Solar	Light energy to electrical energy
Landfill Gas	Kinetic energy (gas movement) and heat energy to mechanical energy to electrical energy
Hydroelectric	Kinetic energy (water movement) to mechanical energy to electrical energy
Fossil Fuel	Heat energy to mechanical energy to electrical energy

CHAPTER 17 REVIEW

1. Nuclear energy and fossil fuel burning are methods of generating electricity. What do they have in common?

    A. They produce heat, which is used to turn a turbine, which then generates electricity.

    B. They produce light, which is used to produce heat.

    C. They produce electrical energy directly.

    D. They produce water which is heated into electricity.

2. Which of the following is an example of the conversion of electromagnetic energy to electrical energy?

    A. chemical battery

    B. nuclear fission

    C. light bulb

    D. solar cell

3. A car uses gasoline for fuel. Gasoline is a kind of fossil fuel. Which of the following correctly describes how gasoline produces energy that your car uses to move?

    A. The car engine causes fossil fuel atoms to fission.

    B. The car engine burns fossil fuels.

    C. The car engine uses electromagnetic radiation to create a current in your car.

    D. Your engine uses geothermal power.

4. What does a transformer do?

    A. It changes the voltage of the energy.

    B. It changes the wavelength of the energy.

    C. It generates electricity.

    D. It moves electricity.

5. A turbine is used to

    A. change the voltage of electricity.

    B. drive a generator.

    C. drive a car.

    D. move electricity.

1. Ⓐ Ⓑ Ⓒ Ⓓ
2. Ⓐ Ⓑ Ⓒ Ⓓ
3. Ⓐ Ⓑ Ⓒ Ⓓ
4. Ⓐ Ⓑ Ⓒ Ⓓ
5. Ⓐ Ⓑ Ⓒ Ⓓ

Chapter 18
Properties of Waves

In previous chapters, you learned a great deal about energy. Now, let find out how it moves from one place to another.

Let's start this investigation by looking at a typical summer day. You probably sleep late (it is summer, after all) and then head down to the beach. You get into the water to cool off and find yourself being pushed backward toward the shoreline. After a nice, refreshing swim, you get out of the water and dry off in the hot sun (don't forget your sunscreen). Later in the day, you head back home. You are probably pretty hungry from all that swimming, so you put something good to eat in the microwave. Next you probably head toward your room and turn on the radio. Your favorite song begins to play, so you dance for a few minutes before sitting down for the evening.

Figure 18.1 Types of Waves

Take a close look at the events of the paragraph above and you'll notice many situations where energy was moving from one place to another. Where? The water waves of the ocean, electromagnetic rays from the sun, microwaves, radiowaves and soundwaves were all **waves** you experienced that day.

A scientific way to describe waves would be to say that they are evidence of energy being transferred through matter or space. For this energy to be transferred, it has to start somewhere. That starting place is called the initial **disturbance** (think of this as a vibration).

THE DISTURBANCE

Sometimes, the disturbance is **mechanical**, which means a physical movement. An example of this would be ocean waves. But where do ocean waves start? Since there is so much ocean, it is hard to tell. Let's isolate a mechanical wave so you can see the disturbance. Get a length of rope about 2 feet long and lay it on the floor. Grab one end of the rope and begin to move it back and forth, while still flat on the ground. What happens? The motion of your hand (the disturbance) results in motion that travels down the length of the rope (the wave).

There is another important type of wave, called the **electromagnetic wave**. An electromagnetic wave is produced by the vibration of an electrically charged particle. A particle with an electric charge is surrounded by an electric field. When the particle vibrates (moves back and forth), the magnetic field around it also vibrates. When both fields are vibrating, an electromagnetic field is created. You can think of this as a wave of energy that moves up and down, and side to side, at the same time. Movement of electromagnetic energy is called **radiation**.

THE MEDIUM

Another major difference between a mechanical and an electromagnetic wave is how they travel. Do they require a medium or not? A **medium** is any matter (solid, liquid, gas or plasma) that has molecules to transport the wave's energy. **Mechanical waves** have to have a medium through which to travel. The waves move out from the initial disturbance by pushing these molecules of matter and disturbing them. Think of a line of dominoes to see how this works.

Figure 18.2 Dominoes

Electromagnetic waves do not require a medium. That means that they can travel through a **vacuum**. A vacuum is a place with almost no matter — like space. Knowing that, I bet you can figure out one huge source of electromagnetic radiation. That's right — our Sun! Table 18.1 shows a few kinds of waves and their medium.

Table 18.1 Kinds of Waves

Wave	Type	Medium Needed?	Usual Media
Sound waves	Mechanical	Yes	Gas, like air
Ocean waves	Mechanical	Yes	Liquid, like water
Seismic waves	Mechanical	Yes	Solid, like earth
Radio waves	Electromagnetic	No	Solid, liquid, gas, plasma, vacuum
Visible light waves	Electromagnetic	No	Liquid, gas, plasma, vacuum

We will look more closely at both sound waves and electromagnetic radiation in a little bit. Right now, let's examine some general properties that are common to both mechanical and electromagnetic waves: amplitude, wavelength and frequency.

AMPLITUDE

Try this: Tie one end of a rope to a doorknob. Make sure the door is closed so you can pull the rope tight to get a straight line. When you pull the rope tight so it forms a straight horizontal line, the rope is in its resting position. Now let the rope leave a little slack. Create waves by moving the end you're holding up and down. You'll probably notice that if you move the rope a short distance up and down, you will make a short wave, but if you move the rope a greater distance it makes a taller wave. You just discovered **amplitude**! The amplitude of a wave is the maximum distance the wave moves from its resting position. You can also think of amplitude as the vibrations from the resting position up and down. And speaking of up and down, the tops of the waves are called **crests**, and the bottoms of the waves are called **troughs**.

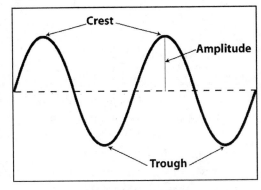

Figure 18.3 Amplitude

As you make different size waves, think about how much energy you put into making smaller waves and how much you put into making larger waves. You have to work much harder to create waves with larger amplitudes than you do to make waves with smaller amplitudes. This is because it takes more energy when you move the rope further from its resting position. Since it takes more energy to make large waves than small waves, you can infer that waves with large amplitudes carry more energy than waves with small amplitudes.

WAVELENGTH AND FREQUENCY

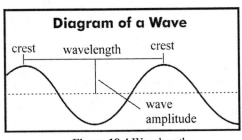

Figure 18.4 Wavelength

Wavelength is the distance from one point on a wave to the same point on the next wave in the "wave train." The **frequency** of a set of waves is how many waves pass by a specified point in a specified amount of time. Most of the time, frequency is described as how many waves pass a given point each second, or as cycles per second. If ten waves pass by a given point per second the frequency is said to be ten cycles per second, which can be written as 10 cps. Another (shorter) way of stating cycles per second is to call the units **Hertz**. One cycle per second is one Hertz (abbreviated as Hz):

$$1 \text{ cps} = 1 \text{ Hz} \qquad \text{Equation 18.1}$$

The higher the frequency of a wave, the more energy it carries. There's also a relationship between the wavelength of a wave and the energy it carries: the shorter the wavelength, the

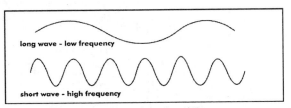

Figure 18.5 Wavelength and Frequency

more energy it carries. This should make sense to you, because when the wavelengths are shorter the waves are closer together; that means that more waves should be able to pass a point in a given amount of time.

SOUND WAVES

A **sound wave** is a mechanical wave produced by a vibrating object. When the object vibrates, it causes the molecules around it to compress (come together) and expand (separate back out). This compression and expansion pattern travels through the medium (solid, liquid or gas) until it reaches your ear. Remember, sound cannot travel through empty space or a vacuum. Sound travels faster through solids than through liquids and gases. Can you test this? You know the answer must be yes or we wouldn't have asked! Stand at two ends of the outside of a brick building. Have a friend gently tap a rhythm on a brick on his or her end. First listen and see if you can hear it in the air. Then put your ear to a brick on your side. You should hear the sound loud and clear when your ear is to the brick…because sound really does travel faster through a solid!

Temperature   As the temperature increases, the speed of sound increases. The motion in the atoms that make up air molecules is faster at hotter temperatures, so it should make sense that sound would move faster.

Humidity   When the air becomes more humid, the speed of sound increases. Why? Humidity is moisture being carried in the air, which makes the air thicker. We already know that sound travels faster through a solid, so it makes sense that the thicker (and more like a solid) air becomes, the faster sound will travel.

THE ELECTROMAGNETIC SPECTRUM

The entire range of electromagnetic waves is called the **electromagnetic spectrum**. Waves in the electromagnetic spectrum include radio waves, microwaves and visible light.

Figure 18.6 arranges the electromagnetic spectrum from long wavelengths to short wavelengths (from right to left). Another way to look at this is that the waves are arranged from low frequency to high frequency.

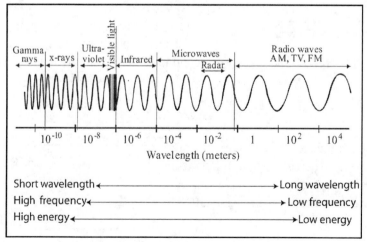

Figure 18.6 The Electromagnetic Spectrum

Now let's talk about each of these waves, starting with the longest ones: radio waves.

Radio Waves: These wavelengths of light are invisible to us, and can range from a few centimeters to more than six football fields long. Radio stations code the sound into radio waves that your radio receives, unscrambles and translates back into sound again.

Figure 18.7 Radio

Microwaves: These invisible waves have a wavelength of only a few millimeters. Your microwave oven uses these waves to heat food. The microwaves generated by the oven's instruments cause the water molecules in the food to vibrate and rotate. It is the movement of the water molecules that heats the food!

Figure 18.8 Microwave

Infrared Waves: These wavelengths are up to a few micrometers in length. Your television's remote control uses a beam of infrared light to change the channel. The electronics in the TV respond to the infrared beam. Your body also radiates infrared light, but of a slightly different wavelength. That is how night vision goggles can see living things moving in the dark.

Figure 18.9 TV Remote

Visible Light Waves: This is the only part of the electromagnetic spectrum that our eyes can see. It's the kind of waves we are most familiar with, but in the grand scheme of the electromagnetic spectrum, it is only very narrow band of wavelengths, from about 0.35 micrometer to 0.9 micrometer. Our eyes sense the different wavelengths in this band as color. A great way to remember in what order the colors are arranged is Roy G Biv. Each letter of this silly name is the first letter of a color in the visible light range.

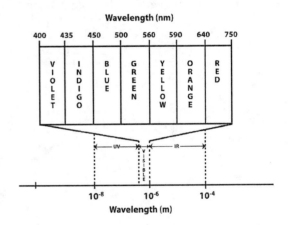

Figure 18.10 Roy G Biv

Figure 18.11 Sunscreen
Blocks UV Light

Ultraviolet Waves: The ozone layer in our Earth's atmosphere helps to protect us from most of the harmful effects of these short wavelength waves. Only some of the Sun's ultraviolet light reaches the ground, and those waves can cause sunburn or even worse, skin cancer. Ultraviolet light penetrates the skin, interacts with molecules and can tear them apart. Use sunscreen!

X-rays: These waves have wavelengths in the nanometer range. They are often used to image bones in a doctor's office. X-rays can be dangerous, so it is best to minimize your exposure to them. That is why the X-ray technician or radiographer covers the parts of your body that are not being X-rayed with a lead apron. This absorbs the radiation.

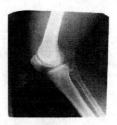

Figure 18.12 X-ray

Gamma Ray Waves: These are the most energetic wavelengths in the electromagnetic spectrum, and they have the shortest wavelengths. Gamma rays are generated by the breaking apart of atomic nuclei. This happens here on Earth, but the majority of gamma rays are produced in space. Gamma radiation is increasingly used by doctors for treating cancer. The "gamma knife" uses the powerful rays to destroy cancerous cells that they are aimed at.

VOLUME AND PITCH

What makes a sound louder or softer? Think about it this way; the **amplitude** is really the wave's **intensity** — the amount of **energy** the wave is carrying. The higher the amplitude, the more energy being carried and the louder, more intense the sound. The intensity, or volume of a sound is measured in units called **decibels**. The higher amplitudes are louder and have a higher number of decibels. Lower amplitudes produce softer sounds with a lower number of decibels.

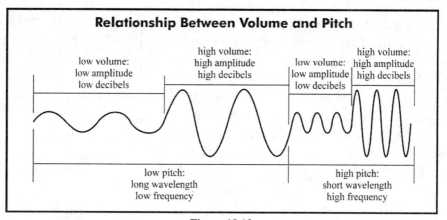

Figure 18.13

THE DOPPLER EFFECT

Let's talk for a moment about how movement affects our perception of waves.

Let's use an example with sound waves to get you started. When a fire engine is not moving, the normal sound of its siren has a certain pitch. When the fire engine is moving towards the observer, the siren sounds as though it has a higher pitch. When the fire engine is moving away, the pitch of the siren sounds lower than normal. The difference in pitch is due to the time it takes for the sound waves to be emitted. If the source is moving away, the beginning of the wave is emitted nearer to the observer than the end of the wave, which stretches the wave, giving it a longer wavelength. If a source is approaching an observer, the opposite is true. Figure 18.14 illustrates the variations in wavelength caused by the relative motion between a source (the fire engine) and an observer.

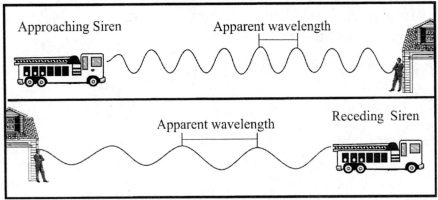

Figure 18.14 Variations in Wavelengths Caused by Motion

So, the Doppler effect can be described as the apparent changes in wavelength of any wave motion caused by the relative position of an observer versus the wave source. OK, that sounds fairly technical, but it's not nearly as difficult as it sounds. Light waves emitted from stars can also exhibit the Doppler effect. White light is a combination of various wavelengths of light, and can be observed when white light is separated by a prism, like a rainbow. (This happens by the

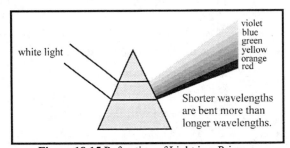

Figure 18.15 Refraction of Light in a Prism

process of refraction, which we'll discuss in Chapter 19.) This combination of wavelengths is called a **spectrum**. We use the spectrum of light from a star or a galaxy to determine if the object is moving away from us. When a star is moving away from the Earth, the light it emits appears redder than it actually is, because its wavelength appears longer. Astronomers call this a **red shift**. Stars moving closer to Earth (there are a few of those, too!) have their light waves shifted toward the blue, or shorter wavelengths of the spectra. This type of shift is a **blue shift**.

CHAPTER 18 REVIEW

1. A raggae band plays all over Atlanta. In which location will the sound of their music travel most quickly to their audience?

    A. jamming on a hot day on Peachtree Street
    B. inside an air conditioned concert hall
    C. at a hot and rainy concert performance in Piedmont Park
    D. practicing in the cool basement of one of the band members

2. How can radio waves be described?
    A. Radio waves are mechanical waves that must move through a medium.
    B. Radio waves are mechanical waves that require no medium.
    C. Radio waves are electromagnetic waves that require no medium.
    D. Radio waves are electromagnetic waves that must move through a medium.

3. Which of the following is NOT an example of a mechanical wave?
    A. sunlight   C. ocean waves
    B. vibrations of a guitar string D. sound waves

4. What is amplitude?
    A. the maximum displacement from the midpoint between the crest and trough
    B. the top of the wave
    C. the horizontal distance the waves travels
    D. the number of waves that pass a specific point in a specific time

5. Which type of wave has the most energy?
    A. a low-frequency wave
    B. a high-frequency wave
    C. a wave length with Hertz
    D. a wave with a magnetic field

1. Ⓐ Ⓑ Ⓒ Ⓓ
2. Ⓐ Ⓑ Ⓒ Ⓓ
3. Ⓐ Ⓑ Ⓒ Ⓓ
4. Ⓐ Ⓑ Ⓒ Ⓓ
5. Ⓐ Ⓑ Ⓒ Ⓓ

Chapter 19
Behavior of Waves

Another thing that is sometimes common to both mechanical and electromagnetic waves is their behavior. By this, we do not mean their table manners, but their **interactions**. Since these waves transfer energy, it makes sense to think that something happens when two waves encounter each other, or some other object. That "something" is a **mode of interaction**. There are several modes of interaction that are common, including reflection, refraction, absorption, transmission and diffraction.

REFLECTION

When a wave hits a barrier, it sometimes bounces back. This bounce is called **reflection**. All waves (sound, light and even water) can be reflected. When sound waves are reflected, we call it an **echo**. It is the light waves reflecting off an object that allows us to see it. When you look up to the sky at night, you see the light waves from the Sun reflecting off the Moon and into your own eyes.

THE LAW OF REFLECTION

Remember the bouncing ball experiments of our first chapters? Let's take that ball out of retirement and bounce it straight toward the ground. When you throw the ball against the smooth surface of the ground, it bounces straight back at you. But what if you threw the ball at an angle? If you throw the ball to the ground at an angle, it will bounce away at an angle.

A beam of light (also known as electromagnetic radiation) behaves essentially the same way! **The Law of Reflection** sums this up by stating that the **angle of incidence** is equal to the **angle of reflection**. What is incidence? For electromagnetic radiation, it's the beam of light falling onto a surface. The diagram to the right shows the key terms and players in the Law of Reflection.

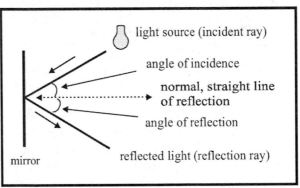

Figure 19.1 Reflection from a Mirror

As you can see in the diagram, the beam of light traveling toward the mirror is the **incident beam**. The beam of light heading away from the mirror is called the **reflected beam**. If you placed an imaginary line perpendicular to the mirror (called the **normal line**), the angle between the incident beam and the normal would be called the angle of incidence, and the angle between the normal and the reflected beam would be called the angle of reflection.

REFRACTION

You may not know this term but you have seen refraction many times. Place a pencil in a half-filled glass of water. Take a look at the pencil on the side and it looks like the pencil has been broken into two pieces. When you pull the pencil out, of course, it's still in one piece. What causes this illusion? When light waves pass from one medium to another (in this case, from water to air) a bending effect called **refraction** takes place.

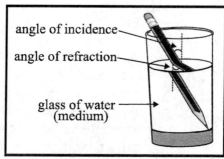

Figure 19.2 Refraction

Think of it this way: the speed of a wave depends on the medium through which it is traveling. When a wave moves from one medium to another, the wave's speed changes…but not all at once! When the wave enters the new medium (at an angle) the part of the wave that enters first begins traveling in a different speed from the rest of the wave. This causes the apparent bend.

Sound waves can also refract, although you can't see them. Think of this: if you are swimming underwater, you can hear loud sounds from above the surface. The sound wave travels at a different speed in water than in air, so voices or other noise may sound different, but you will still hear something.

THE LAW OF REFRACTION

The Law of Refraction shows us the relationship between the incident wave and the refracted wave. It is a mathematical relationship, but we are going to look at it qualitatively (remember, that means without numbers). The Law of Reflection basically tells us that how a beam of incident light bends depends on the medium that it traveled from and the medium that it travels into.

That is because the speed of a light wave depends on the **optical density** of the medium it moves through. How much (and in what direction) light waves will bend, depends on whether the light waves are traveling from a more dense (slow) medium to a less dense (fast) medium, or from a less dense medium to a more dense one.

Angle i is the angle of incidence and **angle r** is the angle of refraction. If light waves move from a less dense (faster) medium to one that is more dense (slower), they will bend toward the normal line. That is the case in Figure 19.3, and you can see that angle r is smaller that angle i.

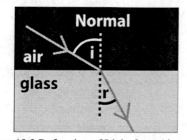

Figure 19.3 Refraction of Light from Air to Glass

On the other hand, if light waves move from a dense (slow) medium to one that is less dense (faster), it will bend away from the normal line. In this case, angle *r* is larger than angle *i*.

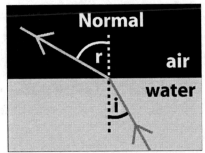

Figure 19.4 Refraction of Light from Water to Air

ABSORPTION

We just looked at what happens when light bounces off of an object, but it's also important to know what happens when light *doesn't* bounce off of objects. When you shine a flashlight, objects closer to you are much brighter than the objects further way. This is because, as the light goes away from the flashlight, some of the energy in the light beam is **absorbed** by the surrounding matter. Light is also **scattered** as it strikes solid particles, like dust, in the air. The further away the light beam goes, the more light is absorbed and scattered by the surrounding air.

As particles of matter absorb the light energy, they turn around and distribute the energy further and further away from the light beam.

Figure 19.5 Absorption of Light

Sound and thermal (heat) waves can also be absorbed. Think of soundproof rooms and oven mitts.

TRANSMISSION

Transmission describes how light passes through matter.

Let's say you're standing at a window at your house. When you look at the glass, you see your **reflection** when light is reflected off the glass from inside the room. When you look through the glass, you can see objects on the outside because light is **transmitted** through the glass. If it is close to midday, you might put your hand on the glass and find it is warmer than the temperature of the room because some of the light energy is **absorbed** by the glass.

Figure 19.6 Experiencing Light

Light travels (is transmitted) through different kinds of matter with varying degrees of "difficulty." Matter through which visible light is easily transmitted is called **transparent**. Water, glass and air are examples of transparent matter. **Translucent** matter allows some light to pass through and **scatters** the rest. Some examples of translucent objects are frosted glass, thin cloth and paper. When matter does not transmit any light, it is called **opaque**. Metal, wood and concrete are examples of opaque matter.

DIFFRACTION

We have now talked about how waves bounce off and go through matter. But there is another phenomenon of waves: how they go around matter. **Diffraction** describes the bending and spreading of waves as they encounter an object or aperture (opening). Diffraction can occur with any type of wave. Ocean waves diffract around piers, buoys and islands. Sound waves diffract around walls, which is why you can still hear your parents yelling for you several rooms away. While diffraction always occurs, it is most noticeable when the wavelength of the wave is of a similar size as the diffraction object or aperture.

Table 19.1 Possible Interactions of a Wave with an Object

Behavior	Description of Wave Motion
Reflection	bounces off the surface at the same angle it hit with
Transmission	travels through the material at the same angle it entered with
Refraction	travels through the material, but at an altered angle
Diffraction	travels through the material until it encounters an obstacle, which it then bends around
Absorption	cannot travel all the way through the material

A COLORFUL CONNECTION

The interaction of light and matter doesn't just determine how much light passes through an object; it also determines the object's color. In the previous chapter, you learned that visible light was a part of the electromagnetic spectrum. Each color of light is determined by a specific wavelength in the small area called the visible light spectrum. Red has the longest wavelength, violet has the shortest and all the others fall in between. When all colors of light are added

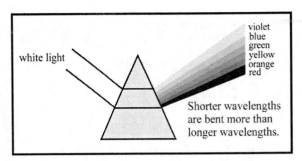

Figure 19.7 Refraction of White Light

together, their combination forms white light. How can we see the colors inside the white light? That is, split apart? You've probably seen a glass prism do this when you were in elementary school...but now it's time to learn how it works.

When white light is refracted, the amount that the light bends depends on its wavelength. Short wavelengths bend more than longer wavelengths. This is why white light separates into different colors during refraction in a prism. Color separation from refraction also makes it possible for you to see rainbows. Instead of glass prisms separating the light, the cause for the refraction is water droplets in our atmosphere!

Your perception of what color an object appears to be is determined by the wavelengths of light that reach your eyes and how your eyes interpret them. Light waves reach your eyes after being reflected off an object or after being transmitted through an object. The object absorbs the colors that you do not see and reflects or transmits the color that you do see.

TO ABSORB AND REFLECT

When white light strikes a colored opaque object, some of the wavelengths within the white light are **absorbed** and some are **reflected**. Only the light that is reflected reaches your eyes, and the wavelength of that light determines the color(s) you see. For example, when you look at your blue jeans, you know they must be reflecting blue light or you would not see them as being blue. You also know that all the other wavelengths of light must be absorbed or you would see them in addition to just the blue. It's important to remember that white light includes all colors of light. So a white object is white because all the colors of light are being reflected. On the other hand, black is the absence of color. When an object appears to be black, all colors of light are being absorbed.

CHAPTER 19 REVIEW

1. What is the angle of incidence equal to when light is reflected?

   A. an acute angle
   B. the angle of reflection
   C. the mode of interaction
   D. the normal line

2. What is the imaginary line perpendicular to a plane of reflection (like a mirror) called?

   A. an incident beam
   B. a reflected beam
   C. the normal line
   D. the angle of incidence

3. Why does the light from a flashlight appear brighter when you shine the light close to the object than when you are far away?

   A. because more light is absorbed by the air
   B. because less light is absorbed by the air
   C. because the light waves become refracted
   D. because the light waves appear at their normal line

4. What does the speed of electromagnetic radiation depend on?

   A. the amount of light
   B. the optical density of the medium through which it is moving
   C. the light's wavelength
   D. the angle of incidence of the light

5. Which of the following wave characteristics allows us to see objects?

   A. reflection   B. refraction   C. amplitude   D. absorption

1. Ⓐ	Ⓑ	Ⓒ	Ⓓ
2. Ⓐ	Ⓑ	Ⓒ	Ⓓ
3. Ⓐ	Ⓑ	Ⓒ	Ⓓ
4. Ⓐ	Ⓑ	Ⓒ	Ⓓ
5. Ⓐ	Ⓑ	Ⓒ	Ⓓ

Unit 2 Review
Physical Science

Use the following image to answer questions 1 – 3.

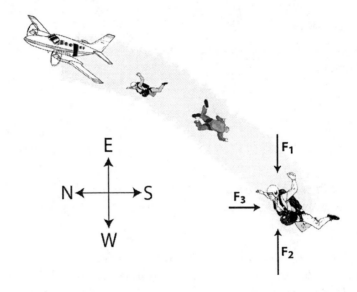

1. What kind of force is represented by F_2?

   A. electromagnetic force

   B. gravitational force

   C. frictional force

   D. tensional force

2. The magnitude of which force will increase as the skydivers fall toward the ground?

   A. F_2

   B. F_3

   C. F_1

   D. F_1 and F_2

3. If a wind starts blowing due south, what will happen?

   A. F_2 will decrease.

   B. F_3 will increase.

   C. F_3 will decrease.

   D. F_1 will increase.

4. Which of the following elements has the greatest atomic mass?
   A. hydrogen
   B. helium
   C. oxygen
   D. neon

5. Noble gases are in Group 18 on the Periodic Table. Which of the following is a chemical property of noble gases?
   A. They are usually solids.
   B. They are very reactive with Group 17 elements.
   C. They are very reactive with Group 1 elements.
   D. They are inert.

6. Most of the elements of the Periodic Table are
   A. gases.
   B. metals.
   C. nonmetals.
   D. metalloids.

7. A(n) _____ is a unit of force.
   A. newton
   B. joule
   C. Kelvin
   D. ampere

8. Velocity includes both speed and
   A. distance.
   B. rate of change.
   C. time.
   D. direction.

The graph to the right shows the motion of a roller coaster from the beginning of the ride to the end. Use the graph to answer question 9.

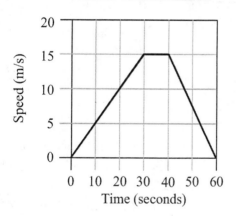

Roller Coaster Motion

9. Identify the motion of the roller coaster during the first 30 seconds, the middle 10 seconds, and the final 20 seconds of the ride.
   A. acceleration, constant speed, negative acceleration
   B. acceleration, stopped, acceleration back to starting point
   C. constant speed up hill, stopped at top of hill, acceleration down hill
   D. constant speed up hill, constant speed at top, constant speed down hill

10. An unbalanced force acts on a body. Identify the change or changes in motion the unbalanced force can produce.
    A. increased speed only
    B. increased or decreased speed only
    C. increased speed and direction change only
    D. increased speed, decreased speed or direction change

11. Which of the following is true regarding the relationship between work and efficiency of a machine?
    A. Since work output is always less than work input, efficiency is always less than 100%.
    B. Since friction increases work output, friction increases the efficiency of machines.
    C. Since work input and work output are always equal, these two quantities do not affect the efficiency of a machine.
    D. Since efficiency of a machine is determined by the ratio of work output to work input, the greater difference in these numbers results in greater efficiency.

12. Which simple machine is represented by a seesaw?

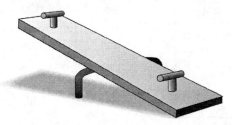

    A. lever   B. wedge   C. inclined   D. screw
                                           plane

13. Which of the following is an example of potential energy?
    A. a rock rolling down a hill   C. a rock at the top of a hill
    B. a rock resting at the bottom of a hill   D. a rock bouncing down a hill

14. Which of the following is an example of kinetic energy?
    A. a baseball flying through the air   C. a baseball in a locker
    B. a baseball in a catcher's mitt   D. a baseball stuck in a house gutter

15. When a substance condenses, it changes from
    A. a liquid to a solid.   C. a gas to a liquid.
    B. a liquid to a gas.   D. a gas to a solid.

16. Mixtures can be separated by physical means. Which is *not* a way to separate mixtures?
    A. evaporation   C. magnetic separation
    B. filtering   D. stirring

17. A substance that can be separated into simpler parts by physical means is
    A. water.   B. salt.   C. salt water.   D. dihydrogen oxide.

18. Carbon dioxide, CO_2, is an example of a(n)
    A. solution.   B. compound.   C. element.   D. mixture.

19. Which of the following does NOT create a mixture?

    A. melting ice   C. salting rice

    B. stirring flour in water   D. making a salad

20. Look at the following blocks of elements as they appear in the Periodic Table. Which two elements would have the most similar chemical properties?

9 F Fluorine 18.998403 2,7	10 Ne Neon 20.179 2,8
17 Cl Chlorine 35.453 2,8,7	18 Ar Argon 39.948 2,8,8

    A. fluorine and chlorine

    B. fluorine and neon

    C. fluorine and argon

    D. chlorine and neon

Post Test 1

Post Test 1   **Answer Sheet**

Name: _____

Section 1

1. Ⓐ Ⓑ Ⓒ Ⓓ
2. Ⓐ Ⓑ Ⓒ Ⓓ
3. Ⓐ Ⓑ Ⓒ Ⓓ
4. Ⓐ Ⓑ Ⓒ Ⓓ
5. Ⓐ Ⓑ Ⓒ Ⓓ
6. Ⓐ Ⓑ Ⓒ Ⓓ
7. Ⓐ Ⓑ Ⓒ Ⓓ
8. Ⓐ Ⓑ Ⓒ Ⓓ
9. Ⓐ Ⓑ Ⓒ Ⓓ
10. Ⓐ Ⓑ Ⓒ Ⓓ
11. Ⓐ Ⓑ Ⓒ Ⓓ
12. Ⓐ Ⓑ Ⓒ Ⓓ
13. Ⓐ Ⓑ Ⓒ Ⓓ
14. Ⓐ Ⓑ Ⓒ Ⓓ
15. Ⓐ Ⓑ Ⓒ Ⓓ
16. Ⓐ Ⓑ Ⓒ Ⓓ
17. Ⓐ Ⓑ Ⓒ Ⓓ
18. Ⓐ Ⓑ Ⓒ Ⓓ
19. Ⓐ Ⓑ Ⓒ Ⓓ
20. Ⓐ Ⓑ Ⓒ Ⓓ
21. Ⓐ Ⓑ Ⓒ Ⓓ

22. Ⓐ Ⓑ Ⓒ Ⓓ
23. Ⓐ Ⓑ Ⓒ Ⓓ
24. Ⓐ Ⓑ Ⓒ Ⓓ
25. Ⓐ Ⓑ Ⓒ Ⓓ
26. Ⓐ Ⓑ Ⓒ Ⓓ
27. Ⓐ Ⓑ Ⓒ Ⓓ
28. Ⓐ Ⓑ Ⓒ Ⓓ
29. Ⓐ Ⓑ Ⓒ Ⓓ
30. Ⓐ Ⓑ Ⓒ Ⓓ

Section 2

31. Ⓐ Ⓑ Ⓒ Ⓓ
32. Ⓐ Ⓑ Ⓒ Ⓓ
33. Ⓐ Ⓑ Ⓒ Ⓓ
34. Ⓐ Ⓑ Ⓒ Ⓓ
35. Ⓐ Ⓑ Ⓒ Ⓓ
36. Ⓐ Ⓑ Ⓒ Ⓓ
37. Ⓐ Ⓑ Ⓒ Ⓓ
38. Ⓐ Ⓑ Ⓒ Ⓓ
39. Ⓐ Ⓑ Ⓒ Ⓓ
40. Ⓐ Ⓑ Ⓒ Ⓓ

41. Ⓐ Ⓑ Ⓒ Ⓓ
42. Ⓐ Ⓑ Ⓒ Ⓓ
43. Ⓐ Ⓑ Ⓒ Ⓓ
44. Ⓐ Ⓑ Ⓒ Ⓓ
45. Ⓐ Ⓑ Ⓒ Ⓓ
46. Ⓐ Ⓑ Ⓒ Ⓓ
47. Ⓐ Ⓑ Ⓒ Ⓓ
48. Ⓐ Ⓑ Ⓒ Ⓓ
49. Ⓐ Ⓑ Ⓒ Ⓓ
50. Ⓐ Ⓑ Ⓒ Ⓓ
51. Ⓐ Ⓑ Ⓒ Ⓓ
52. Ⓐ Ⓑ Ⓒ Ⓓ
53. Ⓐ Ⓑ Ⓒ Ⓓ
54. Ⓐ Ⓑ Ⓒ Ⓓ
55. Ⓐ Ⓑ Ⓒ Ⓓ
56. Ⓐ Ⓑ Ⓒ Ⓓ
57. Ⓐ Ⓑ Ⓒ Ⓓ
58. Ⓐ Ⓑ Ⓒ Ⓓ
59. Ⓐ Ⓑ Ⓒ Ⓓ
60. Ⓐ Ⓑ Ⓒ Ⓓ

GO ON

Georgia 8th Grade CRCT Science – Post Test 1

Session 1

1. Which simple machine is depicted by the modified seesaw in the following diagram? **S8P3c**

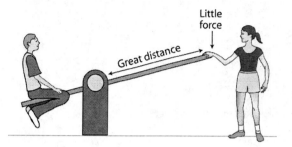

A. a lever

B. a pulley

C. a wedge

D. an inclined plane

2. A student heats a beaker full of water over a low flame. While heating, the student adds 3 grams of salt, which has been measured out on a tared beam balance. He allows the solution to boil until its volume has been reduced by 50%. Then he uses metal tongs to transfer the beaker from the flame to an ice bath. What is the likely result of this series of actions? **S8P1e, S8CS2a**

A. The tongs will melt.

B. The beaker will crack.

C. The beaker will melt.

D. The salt water will combust.

3. Which state of matter is the MOST dense for water? **S8P1d**

A. gaseous water vapor

B. liquid water

C. solid ice

D. Water and ice are equally dense.

4. Table salt is made up of the elements **S8P1f**

A. sodium (Na) and chlorine (Cl).

B. saltium (Sa) and chlorine (Cl).

C. sodium (Sa) and chloride (Ch).

D. nickel (Na) and chloride (Ch).

5. Ross was riding his bike down a hill, and he ran straight into a mailbox. Identify the statement that most closely describes Ross's motion immediately following his collision with the mailbox. **S8P3b**

A. He is thrown forward over the handlebars.

B. He is thrown backwards off the bike.

C. He is thrown sideways off the bike.

D. He is thrown upward into the air.

GO ON

6. A 200 N force, F_1, and a 250 N, F_2, S8P3a, 3b force are applied to the same point at the same time to a large trunk on a frictionless level surface. Which diagram below shows the position of the forces that will give the greatest acceleration to the trunk?

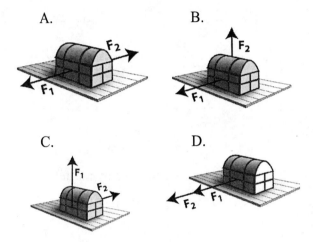

A.

B.

C.

D.

7. *Kinetic* and *potential* are terms that S8P2b describe the expression of the energy of an object. Which of the following statements is true?

   A. All potential energy becomes kinetic energy.

   B. Potential energy is expressed as motion.

   C. All kinetic energy becomes potential energy.

   D. Potential energy is stored.

8. Rust forms by the reaction of iron with S8P1g oxygen to produce iron oxide. An 88 g iron nail rusted. The rusted nail (iron oxide) had a mass of 102 g. Identify the mass of oxygen that reacted in the rusting of the nail.

   A. 14 g

   B. 88 g

   C. 102 g

   D. 200 g

9. Which particle diagram represents one S8P1b pure substance only?

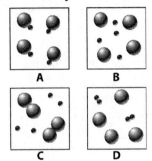

10. Lucas threw a softball up in the air to a S8P3b height of 10 meters. Greg threw a softball up 12 meters. Greg threw the ball higher because

   A. the pull of gravity on the ball was less.

   B. he threw with greater force.

   C. there was less air friction when he threw it.

   D. gravity pulled the ball higher.

11. Which of the following statements best S8CS4c reflects the MOST important factor in a teacher's decision to use Bunsen burners in class?

    A. The teacher must be sure that all the students know how to handle fire.

    B. The teacher must be assured that the Bunsen burners do not use too much energy.

    C. The teacher must be assured that the students will follow instructions.

    D. The teacher must make sure that their school has an emergency exit program in place.

12. You are assigned to identify an S8P1d unknown material in physical science class. The material is malleable and shiny. Which of the following would be the best choice as its identity?

    A. sand

    B. chlorine

    C. carbon

    D. gold

13. The diagram below represents two S8P4b,d waves moving toward each other. They are moving at the same velocity, in the same medium. They have the same wavelength. What is the result of their interaction with particle P?

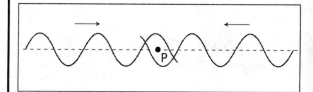

    A. They are reflected by particle P.

    B. They are refracted by particle P.

    C. They cause particle P to move.

    D. They pass particle P, which remains unaffected.

14. Which of the following graphs MOST CLEARLY represents the following information S8CS6c, S8P1f set?

Element	Atomic Radius (picometers)
Lithium	145
Beryllium	105
Boron	85
Carbon	70

A

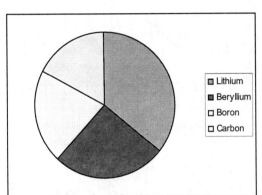

C

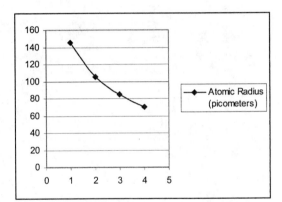

B

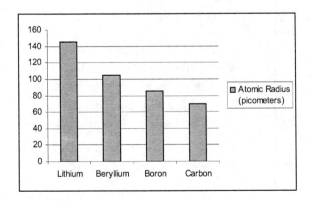

D

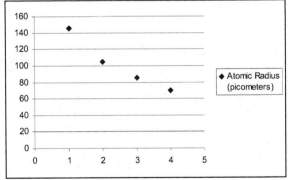

15. Four unknown liquid samples S8CS9b, S8P1d were placed on four different hot plates, and labeled A – D. A thermometer with a maximum temperature of 110°C was placed in each sample. Students were instructed to observe and record the behavior of the samples as they were heated. This data is summarized in the following diagram. Based on the diagram, which sample has the highest boiling point?

A. Sample A

B. Sample B

C. Sample C

D. Sample D

Use the SI unit concept map to answer question 16.

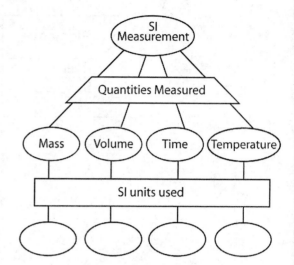

16. The concept map is missing the SI S8CS4c units used to describe standard quantitative measurements. Which sequence shows the appropriate SI base units in the correct order?

A. gram, milliliter, millisecond, Celsius

B. gram, milliliter, second, Celsius

C. gram, liter, second, Kelvin

D. gram, milliliter, second, Kelvin

17. Stacy adds 50 tiny styrofoam balls S8P1c, S8P2d to her 100 mL water sample. She places the sample on the hot plate and heats it until boiling. Describe the motion of the styrofoam balls during this experiment.

A. The motion of the balls would increase as water temperature increased.

B. The motion of the balls would decrease as water temperature increased.

C. The balls would dissolve, so we couldn't see them move.

D. The motion of the balls depends on the size of the sample, not temperature.

GO ON

18. Which process represents a chemical change? S8P1e

    A. melting of ice

    B. corrosion of iron

    C. evaporation of alcohol

    D. crystallization of sugar

19. A recently used hot ceramic teapot is placed on a cold trivet as shown below. Which statement is correct about the sequence of thermal energy transfers? S8P2d

— Trivet

    A. The air transfers energy to the teapot and trivet, and they become cool.

    B. The teapot transfers all of its energy to the air and becomes cool.

    C. The teapot transfers some energy to the trivet and some energy to the air and becomes cool.

    D. The trivet transfers energy to the teapot, and the teapot becomes cool.

20. Which wave interaction is characterized by a wave bending in response to a change in speed? S8P4b

    A. reflection   C. diffraction

    B. refraction   D. interference

Use the data table to answer question 21.

Bubble-blower: Kim	
Trial #	Time(s)
1	1
2	4
3	2
4	4
5	4

21. Debra challenged Kim to a bubble-blowing contest. The point was to see how long a bubble could continue to expand before popping. Kim's data is shown in the table. Upon examining the data, Kim discovered that the value of a common statistical tool was 4. Which statistical tool was it? S8CS3b

    A. the range

    B. the range and the mean

    C. the median

    D. the median and the mode

GO ON

Use the diagram to answer question 22.

22. What process moves thermal energy from the fire in the fireplace to the dog on the rug?   S8P2d

    A. conduction   C. radiation

    B. convection   D. fission

23. In an electric car, a car battery allows an engine to crank. The engine then moves the car from one location to another. Trace the energy transformations shown in the diagram below.   S8P2c

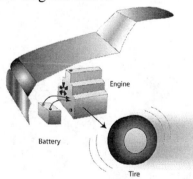

Engine

Battery

Tire

    A. chemical, mechanical, electrical

    B. electrical, chemical, mechanical

    C. chemical, electrical, electrical

    D. chemical, electrical, mechanical

24. Smart glass technologies have become increasingly popular. British scientists recently developed a window glass that helps buildings stay cool. At regular temperatures, the glass allows in both infrared (IR) and ultraviolet (UV) light. But above 29°C, the coating on the glass undergoes a chemical change, causing it to block IR light. What happens to the IR light?   S8P4b, 4d

    A. It is absorbed by the glass.

    B. It is refracted by the glass.

    C. It is reflected by the coating on the glass.

    D. It is refracted by the coating on the glass.

25. When white light is refracted in a prism, which wavelengths are bent the most?   S8P4b, 4c

    A. the shortest ones, violet

    B. the shortest ones, red

    C. the longest ones, violet

    D. the longest ones, red

26. Used tires and other kinds of rubber are ground up and heated and melted into flexible sheets. The finished product is used as flooring for outdoor playgrounds. Characterize this process.   S8P1b, 1e

    A. It is a physical change.

    B. It is a chemical change.

    C. The rubber is transformed from a mixture into its elemental form.

    D. The rubber is transformed from a pure substance into a mixture.

GO ON

27. What characteristic do all waves share? S8P4a

   A. All waves move matter.

   B. All waves transfer energy.

   C. All waves can move through a vacuum.

   D. All waves travel at 3.0×10^8 m/s.

28. Describe the result of the following process: A piece of cloth burns. S8P1d

   A. a physical change only

   B. a chemical change only

   C. a physical and chemical change

   D. a chemical property only

29. Which of the following is the BEST example of potential energy? S8P2b

   A. a fire

   B. a match

   C. a balloon

   D. thunder

30. Loosening the strings of a guitar will cause the pitch to become S8P4e

   A. softer.

   B. louder.

   C. lower.

   D. higher.

SESSION 2

31. Which of the following pH values describes a strong acid? S8P1d

    A. 1

    B. 4

    C. 7

    D. 13

32. Which of the following cannot be found on the Periodic Table? S8P1f

    A. aluminum chloride

    B. nitrogen

    C. titanium

    D. magnesium

33. An electric circuit allows electricity to flow between two poles: a negative pole and a positive pole. What is deficient at the positive pole? S8P5c

    A. protons

    B. neutrons

    C. electrons

    D. atoms

34. Cerise is measuring the length of a strip of aluminum, approximately the same size as her thumb. Which of the following is the most appropriate way to express the measurement? S8CS3d

    A. 0.7 mm

    B. 7 cm

    C. 70 dm

    D. 7000 dam

35. Which two molecules contain an equal number of atoms? S8P1a

    C_2H_6 $KMnO_4$ H_2SO_4 C_2H_3OH

    A. H_2SO_4 and C_2H_3OH

    B. C_2H_6 and $KMnO_4$

    C. $KMnO_4$ and H_2SO_4

    D. C_2H_6 and C_2H_3OH

36. Lead is a bluish-white metal that will burn in air to produce lead (II) oxide. It is highly malleable and was used by the Romans to make pipes to carry water ("plumbing" is taken from the Latin name for lead "plum bum"). It has a relatively low melting point of 327°C and an atomic weight of 207.2 amu. Which property of lead is a chemical property? S8P1d

    A. high malleability

    B. burns in air

    C. low melting point

    D. atomic weight is 207.2 amu

37. In order to determine the velocity of an object, what measurements must be made? S8P3a, 3b

    A. time and distance

    B. time, distance and mass

    C. time, distance and direction

    D. time, distance and volume

38. An analogy can be drawn between   S8P2b,5b
    the work done by an electric current
    flowing through an electrical appliance and
    the work done by water flowing over a
    waterfall. In such an analogy, identify the
    property of the electric current that is
    analogous to the rate of flow of water over
    the fall.

    A. power

    B. voltage

    C. amperage

    D. resistance

39. Identify the types of fields that   S8P5a,c
    interact to produce motion in an
    electric generator.

    A. an electrical field and a gravitational field

    B. a magnetic field and an electrical field

    C. two electrical fields

    D. two magnetic fields

40. Alan constructs a circuit that has two   S8P5c
    1.5 V batteries arranged in series.
    These batteries power a single light bulb.
    What will happen if Alan adds another load
    in series?

    A. The resistance of the circuit has increased,
       so more current will flow.

    B. The voltage of the circuit has increased,
       so more current will flow.

    C. The resistance of the circuit has
       decreased, so less current will flow.

    D. The resistance of the circuit has
       increased, so less current will flow.

41. The loss or gain of which subatomic   S8P1a,d
    particle has the greatest effect on
    chemical reactivity?

    A. electron

    B. proton

    C. neutron

    D. nucleon

Answer questions 42 – 43 based on the summary of the experiment.

A group of students wanted to find out how heat affects the rate of chemical reactions. They used hydrogen peroxide, which breaks down into oxygen and water, for their experiment. The students measured how long it took to obtain 50 mL of oxygen when the hydrogen peroxide was heated at different temperatures. They used the same amount of hydrogen peroxide for each test and measured the time it took for each sample to produce 50 mL of oxygen. The data follows:

Temperature (°C)	Time (minutes)
10	33
20	16
30	8
40	4.1
50	2.1

42. What is a necessary safety precaution when performing this experiment? S8CS2b,c

   A. Follow animal safety guidelines.

   B. Follow the scientific method.

   C. Follow heat and fire safety rules.

   D. Safety rules are not necessary for this experiment.

43. What were some of the tools most likely used during this experiment? S8CS4b

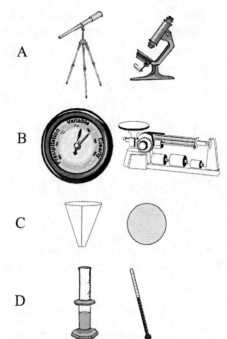

   A

   B

   C

   D

44. When energy is transformed from one form to another, some of the energy is lost in the form of S8P2c, d

   A. mechanical energy.

   B. hydrogen gas.

   C. water.

   D. thermal energy.

45. Rita obtains an unknown liquid   S8P2d
sample from her teacher. It has a mass
of 7 grams, and it fills a graduated cylinder to
Level A. She is given the densities of the
following four liquids to help her identify the
sample. Which one is it?

	g/mL
water	1.00
vegetable oil	0.93
honey	1.42
gasoline	0.70

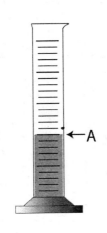

←A

A. water

B. vegetable oil

C. honey

D. gasoline

46. Which of the following produces   S8P2c
energy from processes that do not
involve a chemical change?

A. a bonfire

B. a fossil fuel power plant

C. a solar cell

D. a car

47. The speed of an object increases 10   S8P3a
m/s over 10 seconds. What is its
acceleration?

A. 0 m/s^2

B. 1 m/s^2

C. 10 m/s^2

D. 100 m/s^2

48. Which of the following is a source of   S8P2b
potential energy that could release
radiant energy?

A. a diamond

B. a salt water

C. a neutron

D. a match

49. Which of the following is true of   S8P5a, 5c
gravity on Earth?

A. All matter exerts a force of gravity.

B. Only very large pieces of matter can
exert gravity.

C. Earth pulls matter toward itself, and matter pushes Earth away.

D. Earth pushes matter away, and matter
pulls Earth toward itself.

GO ON

50. Which of the following experimental set-ups would be the best to use if a scientist were trying to confirm the speed of light in space? S8P4a,d

    A. A laser is assembled in a vacuum chamber.

    B. A laser is assembled in a chamber filled with steel.

    C. A laser is assembled in chamber filled with humid air.

    D. A laser is assembled in a chamber filled with dry air.

Use the following information to answer questions 51 – 52.

Liquid hydrogen peroxide undergoes a chemical reaction, decomposing into hydrogen gas and oxygen gas. The reaction is as follows:

$$H_2O_2(l) \longrightarrow H_2(g) + O_2(g)$$

51. Which of the following has the greatest amount of molecular motion? S8P1c

    A. H_2O_2 molecules

    B. H_2O_2 atoms

    C. H_2 and O_2 molecules

    D. H_2 and O_2 atoms

52. If the reaction began with 50 grams of hydrogen peroxide, what is the product of the decomposition? S8P1g

    A. 20 grams of H_2 and O_2.

    B. 50 grams of H_2 and O_2.

    C. 50 grams of O_2, because it is the heavier element.

    D. Zero grams, because gas has no mass.

53. Which of the following has both wavelength (λ) and amplitude (A) labeled correctly? S8P4f

A.

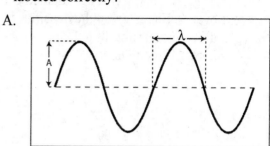

B.

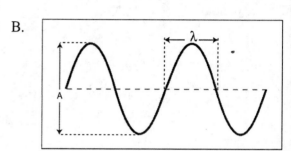

C.

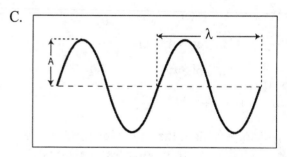

D.

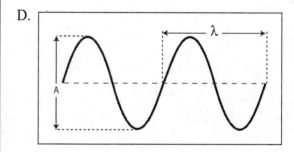

54. What is one advantage of a parallel circuit over a series circuit? S8P5b

A. It lasts longer.

B. It can handle more loads.

C. Flow of current stops when one switch is opened.

D. Its resistance decreases as more loads are added.

55. Which statement correctly describes the difference between an atom and a molecule? S8P1a

A. An atom consists of one or more molecules chemically joined together.

B. An atom is the result of the physical separation of molecules.

C. A molecule consists of one or more atoms chemically joined together.

D. A molecule is one or more atoms physically joined together.

56. The human eye could not see the green color of a leaf without S8P4c

A. red light being reflected from the leaf's surface.

B. red light being absorbed by the leaf's surface.

C. green light being reflected by the leaf's surface.

D. green light being refracted by the leaf's surface.

57. Which of the following is an example of an electromagnetic wave? S8P4a

A. gamma rays

B. electrons

C. nuclei

D. sound waves

58. A wheelbarrow is used to roll loads of dirt from the back yard to the front yard of Nellie's house. Three paths of equal distance and slope are available. Which would be the best choice, to reduce the amount of work that Nellie must do? S8P3b,c

A. The grass path.

B. The gravel path.

C. The concrete path.

D. Work will be the same over all paths, because the distance is equal.

59. Two magnets are brought together in all possible orientations. Which arrangement will produce the greatest repulsive force? S8P5c

A. NSSN

B. NSNS

C. SNNS

D. A and C will be produce equally repulsive forces.

60. Which of the following explains the   S8P5a
    effect of gravity in space?

    A. There is no gravity in space.

    B. Gravity in space will be determined by
       the closeness of matter with a large
       mass.

    C. Gravity in space will be determined by
       the closeness of matter with a small
       mass.

    D. Gravity in space will be determined by
       the location of electromagnetic radia-
       tion.

Post Test 2

Post Test 2   **Answer Sheet**

Name: _____

Section 1

1. Ⓐ Ⓑ Ⓒ Ⓓ
2. Ⓐ Ⓑ Ⓒ Ⓓ
3. Ⓐ Ⓑ Ⓒ Ⓓ
4. Ⓐ Ⓑ Ⓒ Ⓓ
5. Ⓐ Ⓑ Ⓒ Ⓓ
6. Ⓐ Ⓑ Ⓒ Ⓓ
7. Ⓐ Ⓑ Ⓒ Ⓓ
8. Ⓐ Ⓑ Ⓒ Ⓓ
9. Ⓐ Ⓑ Ⓒ Ⓓ
10. Ⓐ Ⓑ Ⓒ Ⓓ
11. Ⓐ Ⓑ Ⓒ Ⓓ
12. Ⓐ Ⓑ Ⓒ Ⓓ
13. Ⓐ Ⓑ Ⓒ Ⓓ
14. Ⓐ Ⓑ Ⓒ Ⓓ
15. Ⓐ Ⓑ Ⓒ Ⓓ
16. Ⓐ Ⓑ Ⓒ Ⓓ
17. Ⓐ Ⓑ Ⓒ Ⓓ
18. Ⓐ Ⓑ Ⓒ Ⓓ
19. Ⓐ Ⓑ Ⓒ Ⓓ
20. Ⓐ Ⓑ Ⓒ Ⓓ
21. Ⓐ Ⓑ Ⓒ Ⓓ

22. Ⓐ Ⓑ Ⓒ Ⓓ
23. Ⓐ Ⓑ Ⓒ Ⓓ
24. Ⓐ Ⓑ Ⓒ Ⓓ
25. Ⓐ Ⓑ Ⓒ Ⓓ
26. Ⓐ Ⓑ Ⓒ Ⓓ
27. Ⓐ Ⓑ Ⓒ Ⓓ
28. Ⓐ Ⓑ Ⓒ Ⓓ
29. Ⓐ Ⓑ Ⓒ Ⓓ
30. Ⓐ Ⓑ Ⓒ Ⓓ

Section 2

31. Ⓐ Ⓑ Ⓒ Ⓓ
32. Ⓐ Ⓑ Ⓒ Ⓓ
33. Ⓐ Ⓑ Ⓒ Ⓓ
34. Ⓐ Ⓑ Ⓒ Ⓓ
35. Ⓐ Ⓑ Ⓒ Ⓓ
36. Ⓐ Ⓑ Ⓒ Ⓓ
37. Ⓐ Ⓑ Ⓒ Ⓓ
38. Ⓐ Ⓑ Ⓒ Ⓓ
39. Ⓐ Ⓑ Ⓒ Ⓓ
40. Ⓐ Ⓑ Ⓒ Ⓓ

41. Ⓐ Ⓑ Ⓒ Ⓓ
42. Ⓐ Ⓑ Ⓒ Ⓓ
43. Ⓐ Ⓑ Ⓒ Ⓓ
44. Ⓐ Ⓑ Ⓒ Ⓓ
45. Ⓐ Ⓑ Ⓒ Ⓓ
46. Ⓐ Ⓑ Ⓒ Ⓓ
47. Ⓐ Ⓑ Ⓒ Ⓓ
48. Ⓐ Ⓑ Ⓒ Ⓓ
49. Ⓐ Ⓑ Ⓒ Ⓓ
50. Ⓐ Ⓑ Ⓒ Ⓓ
51. Ⓐ Ⓑ Ⓒ Ⓓ
52. Ⓐ Ⓑ Ⓒ Ⓓ
53. Ⓐ Ⓑ Ⓒ Ⓓ
54. Ⓐ Ⓑ Ⓒ Ⓓ
55. Ⓐ Ⓑ Ⓒ Ⓓ
56. Ⓐ Ⓑ Ⓒ Ⓓ
57. Ⓐ Ⓑ Ⓒ Ⓓ
58. Ⓐ Ⓑ Ⓒ Ⓓ
59. Ⓐ Ⓑ Ⓒ Ⓓ
60. Ⓐ Ⓑ Ⓒ Ⓓ

GO ON

Session 1

1   When liquids of different densities   S8P1d
    are mixed together, they will some-   S8CS6c
    times separate and form layers. Based
    on the phases indicated below, what can you
    infer about the density of these liquids?

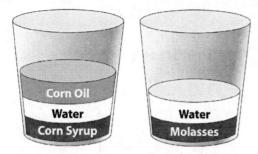

A. Water is less dense than corn oil.

B. Water is more dense than molasses.

C. Corn oil is less dense than molasses.

D. Corn syrup is more dense than molasses.

2. Clara wants to determine the volume   S8P1d,
    of an ice cube. She places the cube into   S8CS2b
    a graduated cylinder and waits for it to melt.
    Is this an accurate way of determining the
    volume of the ice cube?

A. Yes. The melted ice cube will be the same
    volume as the frozen ice cube.

B. No. The melted ice cube has a smaller
    volume than the frozen ice cube, because
    liquid water is denser than solid water.

C. No. Water vapor will be lost to the air
    during melting, which will change the
    measured volume of the two states.

D. Yes. Even though the volume of water in
    ice and liquid form is different, it is not
    enough to be measureable.

3. Sodium has a violent exothermic   S8P1e,
    reaction with water, producing   S8CS10c
    hydrogen gas and a clear, aqueous sodium
    hydroxide solution. What else is produced in
    this reaction?

A. gamma rays

B. heat

C. ice

D. electricity

4. A nuclear power plant uses the fission   S8P2c
    process to generate heat, which turns
    turbines, which in turn create electricity. A
    solar cell absorbs radiant solar energy and
    turns it directly into electricity. A
    hydroelectric power station uses the
    movement of water to turn turbines, which in
    turn create electricity. Electricity is generated
    from each of these energy sources. Which
    does not involve the use of mechanical
    energy?

A. nuclear power generation

B. solar power generation

C. hydroelectric power generation

D. All of these methods involve the use of
    mechanical energy.

5. A science class is conducting a   S8CS2a, 2b, 2c, 4c
laboratory activity that involves observing a chemical reaction. Each pair of students is given a flask closed with a rubber stopper and containing an unknown liquid. The students are told that the stopper needs to stay on the flask because the liquid inside will burn skin. Students are also told to keep their aprons and goggles on throughout the lab. Students will observe the chemical reaction that takes place when, after shaking the flask, the liquid is mixed with the air sitting above it. Which of the following actions displays safe laboratory procedures?

A. Instead of shaking the flask, Adam and Shalandra turn the flask upside down and balance it on the rubber stopper to ensure that the liquid mixes sufficiently with the air.

B. After completing the experiment, Mandy and Raul carefully remove the stopper and waft the fumes produced by the liquid to try and determine its identity.

C. Alka and Travis take turns shaking the flask throughout the experiment. They record their observation and return the flask to a location designated by the teacher at the end of the lab.

D. Since the rubber stopper is going to remain in the flask throughout the experiment, Matias and Tara take their goggles off so that they can see the reaction more clearly.

6. The angle of the stirring rod in the   S8P4b, 4d
beaker appears to change at the surface of the water. This phenomenon is explained by which property of light?

A. scattering

B. diffraction

C. reflection

D. refraction

7. Which process represents a chemical   S8P1e
change?

A. melting of ice

B. corrosion of iron

C. evaporation of alcohol

D. crystallization of sugar

8. What is the best way to heat a beaker of water on a Bunsen burner? **S8CS2b**

   A. Place the beaker on a covered tripod over the flame. Heat for 5 minutes, then add the water.

   B. Add water and boiling stones to the beaker, place on the covered tripod stand and then heat until boiling.

   C. Fill the beaker with water and boiling stones, then use metal tongs to hold it over the flame.

   D. Fill the beaker with water and boiling stones, then hold it over the flame using your hands.

9. In the following concept map, some items are missing. Which of the following is an item that could appear as a non-metal? **S8P1f**

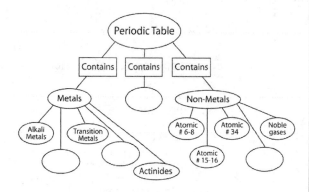

   A. alkali earth metals

   B. metalloids

   C. halogens

   D. lanthanides

10. Jill places a message in a bottle and drops it off a cliff, into the ocean. When does the bottle have the greatest kinetic energy? **S8P2b**

    A. when Jill holds the bottle in her hand, just before dropping it

    B. just after Jill releases the bottle

    C. just before the bottle hits the surface of the water

    D. when it is floating on the water

11. Shaquille has two test tubes full of water. He boils the water in Test Tube A. He adds green food coloring to the water in Test Tube B. In which test tube did a chemical change take place? **S8P1e**

    A. Test Tube A

    B. Test Tube B

    C. in both test tubes

    D. in neither test tube

12. Mark is flying a kite on the beach. The kite and Mark are facing due west. A sudden gust of wind forces Mark to turn toward the right. What direction is the wind gusting from? **S8P3b**

    A. The wind is blowing in from the south.

    B. The wind is blowing in from the north.

    C. The wind is blowing in from the east.

    D. The wind is blowing in from the west.

172

13. A pot holder is used to pick up hot   S8P2d
objects. What is the function of the pot
holder?

    A. It absorbs heat.

    B. It reflects heat.

    C. It transmits heat.

    D. It eliminates heat.

Use the figure to answer question 14.

14. Three distinct modes of heat transfer   S8P2d
are happening in the diagram. Which process
circulates energy inside the heating pan of
liquid?

    A. radiation

    B. convection

    C. circulation

    D. conduction

15. A beam of light is directed through   S8P4b, 4d
one material into another. Which of the
following factors will have the GREATEST
effect on the degree to which the light is
refracted?

    A. the difference in density between the two
    materials

    B. the difference in mass between the two
    materials

    C. the distance that the light has to travel in
    each medium

    D. the color change of the light

16. Which of the following scenarios   S8P3b, S8P3c
would make the box EASIEST to
move?

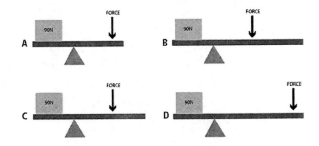

17. Carlos leaves four items pressed   S8P1e
between the folds of a wet paper
towel: a tack, a nail, a staple and a paper clip.
If only the nail rusts, what does Carlos know
about the nail?

    A. The nail is made of steel, but the other
    items are not.

    B. The nail is made of a metal, but the other
    items are not.

    C. The nail is made of a different material
    that the other items.

    D. The other items have been painted.

Use the data table to answer question 18.

Element	Density (g/cm³)
tungsten (W)	19.25
iron (Fe)	7.86
magnesium (Mg)	1.74
aluminum (Al)	2.7

18. Archie has a 4-gram sample of an   S8P1d
unknown metal. His job in lab is to
figure out which metal it is. Using water
displacement, he determines that his sample
has a volume of about 0.5 cm³. Which metal
is Archie's sample?

  A. tungsten

  B. iron

  C. magnesium

  D. aluminum

19. Martina has three test tubes, each   S8CS2b
containing a different clear liquid.
One is rubbing alcohol, one is water and one
is corn syrup. What would be the BEST way
for Martina to determine which one was
rubbing alcohol?

  A. Look at all three samples under the
microscope.

  B. Remove top of the test tube and waft the
scent of the vial toward her nose.

  C. Ignite all three samples.

  D. Send all the samples off for analysis.

20. Which of the following pieces of   S8CS4b
equipment would you use to heat a
liquid on a hot plate?

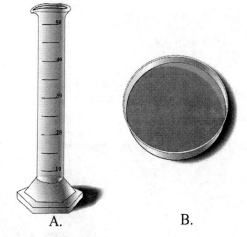

A.   B.

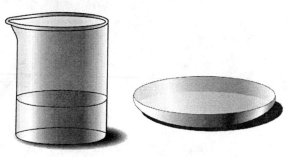

C.   D.

GO ON

21. Which of the equations below is the correct dimensional equation to convert 55 mph to feet/sec?   S8CS3a

    A. $\dfrac{55\ mi}{hr} \cdot \dfrac{1\ mi}{5{,}280\ ft} \cdot \dfrac{1\ hr}{60\ min} \cdot \dfrac{1\ min}{60\ sec}$

    B. $\dfrac{55\ mi}{hr} \cdot \dfrac{5{,}280\ ft}{1\ mi} \cdot \dfrac{1\ hr}{60\ min} \cdot \dfrac{1\ min}{60\ sec}$

    C. $\dfrac{55\ mi}{hr} \cdot \dfrac{1\ mi}{5{,}280\ ft} \cdot \dfrac{60\ min}{1\ hr} \cdot \dfrac{1\ min}{60\ sec}$

    D. $\dfrac{55\ mi}{hr} \cdot \dfrac{1\ mi}{5{,}280\ ft} \cdot \dfrac{60\ min}{1\ hr} \cdot \dfrac{60\ sec}{1\ min}$

22. The circuit below represents the wiring in a power strip. Identify the way the circuit is wired and, if one device breaks, the effect on the other devices.   S8P5b

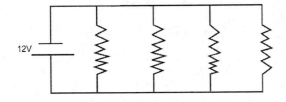

    A. wired in parallel; other devices remain on

    B. wired in parallel; other devices turn off

    C. wired in series; other devices remain on

    D. wired in series; other devices turn off

23. A bowling ball with a mass of 5.44 kg and a soccer ball with a mass of 0.43 kg are dropped from a 15 m platform. Identify the correct description of the acceleration of the bowling ball and the force with which it hits the ground, with respect to the soccer ball.   S8P3a,b

    A. The force of the bowling ball is greater, and its acceleration is greater.

    B. The force of the bowling ball is greater, and its acceleration is the same.

    C. The force of the bowling ball is the same, and its acceleration is greater.

    D. The force of the bowling ball is the same, and its acceleration is the same.

24. Where are the halogens in the diagram below? S8P1f

PERIODIC TABLE OF THE ELEMENTS

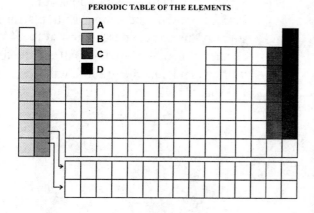

- [ ] A
- [ ] B
- [ ] C
- [ ] D

A. A

B. B

C. C

D. D

25. Refer to the equation below. It gives off heat as a product. It is a/an _____ reaction. S8P1e, S8CS10c

$$P_4 + 5O_2 \longrightarrow P_4O_{10}$$

A. exothermic

B. neutralization

C. endothermic

D. decomposition

26. Which of the following correctly places the phases of water in order from the most dense to the least dense? S8P1b, c

A. solid, liquid, gas, plasma

B. plasma, gas, liquid, solid

C. liquid, solid, gas, plasma

D. liquid, gas, plasma, solid

27. In the experiment shown in the diagram below, a student is to record how much time elapses from the time the Bunsen burner is lit until the wax on the end of each rod begins to melt. Which of the following would be the best title for a laboratory report describing this experiment? S8CS7b

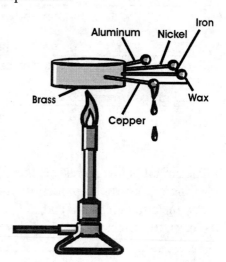

A. Rate of Radiation of a Candle Flame

B. Generation of Electric Currents in Various Metals

C. Rate of Thermal Conduction in Various Metals

D. Determining Melting Point in Wax

28. Which substance represents a compound?

    S8P1b

    A. C

    B. O_2

    C. CO_2

    D. Co

29. Mark adds liquid water to an ice tray and places it in the freezer. What happens?

    S8P2d

    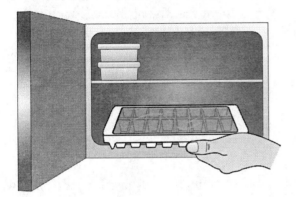

    A. Thermal energy flows from the higher-energy phase (water) to the lower-energy phase (cold air).

    B. Thermal energy flows from the higher-energy phase (cold air) to the lower-energy phase (water).

    C. Cold radiates from the cold air into the warm water.

    D. The insulation of the ice tray keeps the temperature from changing much.

30. A solution is made by dissolving 10 g of salt in 500 g of water. Identify the mass of the resulting solution.

    S8P1g

    A. 500 g

    B. more than 500 g but less than 510 g

    C. 510 g

    D. more than 510 g

STOP

SESSION 2

31. Increasing the current applied to an   S8P5c
    electromagnet will affect which of
    the following?

    A. the voltage delivered by the
       electromagnet

    B. the magnetic field exerted by the
       electromagnet

    C. the mass of the electromagnet

    D. the nuclear force delivered by the
       electromagnet

32. A wet cell battery is an example of   S8P2b, c
    stored potential energy. Once
    connected to a load, the stored energy is
    converted. Describe the conversion of
    energy that results in the movement of the
    hands in a battery-powered clock.

    A. chemical to electrical to mechanical

    B. chemical to thermal to electrical

    C. electrical to thermal to mechanical

    D. chemical to electrical to thermal

33. Which of the following is able to   S8P2a, c
    convert all the thermal energy
    produced into useful work?

    A. nuclear power reactor

    B. gasoline engine

    C. stovetop range

    D. none of the above

34. How long does it take to accelerate an   S8P3a
    object from 10 m/s to 18 m/s if the
    acceleration over that period was 2 m/s^2?

    A. 16 s

    B. 20 s

    C. 9 s

    D. 4 s

35. Sound waves cause molecules to   S8P4d
    vibrate and bump into one another. For
    sound to travel, there must be molecules
    which can be made to vibrate. The closer
    together the molecules are, the faster the
    sound is able to travel. This explains why

    A. sound travels faster in steel than in water.

    B. sound travels faster in outer space than in
       air.

    C. sound travels faster in air than in water.

    D. sound travels faster in water than in
       steel.

GO ON

Use the graph below to answer question 36.

Changing the States of Water

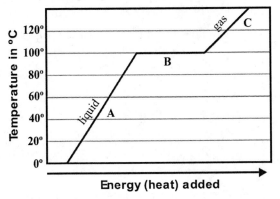

36. Why does the temperature remain   S8P2d, a
    constant during section B of the
    graph?

    A. During section B, the temperature of the
       liquid phase cancels out the temperature
       of the gas phase.

    B. During section B, energy is neither added
       nor removed.

    C. During section B, the energy added is
       being used to change from a liquid phase
       to a gas phase.

    D. During section B, a solid of constant tem-
       perature is formed as an intermediate
       phase between liquid and gas.

37. Iron is continuously heated,   S8P4a,c, S8CS6b
    and the light emitted is
    observed at several temperatures. As the
    temperature increases, the spectrum given
    off by the iron changes. The following table
    gives temperature and spectrum data for
    three temperatures. Predict the spectrum
    observed at 3000K.

Temperature (Kelvin)	Observed Spectrum
1000	red
1500	red, orange, yellow
2000	red, orange, yellow, green
3000	?

    A. red only

    B. red, orange, yellow, green

    C. red, orange, yellow, green, blue, violet

    D. violet only

38. Find the amount of work done when   S8P3c
    30 N of force is used to lift a box 400
    cm.

400 cm—

30N—

    A. 7.5 Joules

    B. 13.3 Joules

    C. 120 Joules

    D. 12,000 Joules

When two light nuclei are forced to fuse, they form a heavier nucleus. During this process, a large amount of energy is produced. When the process is conducted at room temperatures and standard pressures, it is called cold fusion.

In 1989, Stanley Pons and Martin Fleischmann announced at a press conference that they had produced cold fusion one time in their laboratory. All over the world, scientists rushed to their labs to try and duplicate the experiment. In the end, no one was successful. Pons and Fleischmann were harshly criticized in the science community.

39. Why were Pons and Fleischmann criticized by the scientific community? S8CS7b, 8a, 10a

A. Because they tried to produce cold fusion.

B. Because they lied about producing cold fusion.

C. Because their results were not reproducible.

D. Because cold fusion is not possible.

40. Which of the following best explains the difference between melting and boiling points? S8P1c, e

A. The melting point is the temperature at which a gas becomes plasma. The boiling point is the temperature at which a gas becomes a liquid.

B. The boiling point is the temperature at which a liquid becomes a gas. The melting point is the temperature at which a solid becomes a liquid.

C. The melting point is the temperature at which a liquid becomes a gas. The boiling point is the temperature at which a solid becomes a liquid.

D. The boiling point is the temperature at which a solid becomes a gas. The melting point is the temperature at which a gas becomes a liquid.

41. Tammy's room contains a lamp, a hair dryer, a radio and a TV. She uses an ohmmeter to determine that the overall resistance of the circuit increases as she plugs each appliance in. What kind of wiring is the circuitry in Tammy's house? S8P5b

A. series

B. parallel

C. mixed

D. direct

42. Examine the following diagram. S8CS2a, b
Which student is using a correct
procedure to heat the test tube, and why?

A. Student A is using correct procedure: she
is holding the mouth of the test tube away
from her, and she is wearing her goggles.

B. Student B is using correct procedure: she
is observing the reaction in the test tube
very closely.

C. Neither student is following safe procedure: a hot plate should always be used in
place of a Bunsen Burner.

D. Both students are following acceptable
procedures.

43. Lara navigates her kayak down S8P3a, S8CS3f
a stretch of the Chattahoochee
River in 15 minutes. Her rate of speed over
the course of the trip is 8 km/hr. How far has
she traveled?

A. 0.12 km

B. 1.2 km

C. 2 km

D. 120 km

44. A submarine uses sonar to S8P4e, S8CS3f
measure the distance between
itself and other underwater objects. It sends
out a sound wave, then records the echo that
is reflected back by an underwater object.
The speed of sound in water is about 1500
m/s. How far away is an object whose echo
takes 5 seconds to return?

A. 300 meters

B. 7500 meters

C. 3750 meters

D. 15000 meters

45. What does the following diagram S8P4a, f
illustrate?

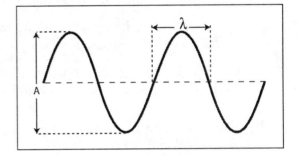

A. the amplitude of a wave and the
wavelength of a wave

B. the amplitude of a wave and half the
wavelength of a wave

C. twice the amplitude of a wave and the
wavelength of a wave

D. twice the amplitude of a wave and half
the wavelength of a wave

GO ON

46. Sheera has a 4-mg sample of neon. Which of the following containers would it be found in? _{S8P1c, 1e}

    A. a test tube

    B. a sealed glass vial

    C. a beaker

    D. a weighing dish

47. The mechanical advantage of a lever is determined by which of the following? _{S8P3c}

    A. the ratio of the length of the lifting arm to the height of the fulcrum

    B. the ratio of the length of the resistance arm to the height of the fulcrum

    C. the ratio of the length of the lifting arm to the length of the resistance arm

    D. the ratio of the length of the resistance arm to the length of the lifting arm

48. When applied to sound waves, the Doppler effect describes the perceived change in pitch with the movement of the sound source. How does the Doppler effect describe the movement of stars? _{S8P4e, f}

    A. as the perceived change in frequency of the light emitted from a moving star

    B. as the perceived change in amplitude of the light emitted from a moving star

    C. as the perceived change in sound waves emitted by a moving star

    D. as the perceived change in distance of a stationary star

49. What does a molecule have that an atom does not? _{S8P1a}

    A. a nucleus

    B. protons

    C. chemical bonds

    D. chemical properties

50. Which of the following scenarios would produce the most noticeable diffraction? _{S8P4b}

    A. A radio is played in front of a sieve.

    B. A water wave crashes to shore.

    C. A laser beam is aimed at a Frisbee.

    D. Your mom calls to you from three rooms away.

51. The surface gravity of a planet is the gravitational acceleration experienced at that planet's surface. The following table shows the surface gravitational acceleration of four planets. On which planet will you weigh the most? _{S8P5a}

Earth	9.81 m/s^2
Mars	3.69 m/s^2
Venus	8.87 m/s^2
Neptune	11.15 m/s^2

    A. Mars

    B. Venus

    C. Neptune

    D. The distance of the planet from the Sun is needed to answer the question.

52. The atoms of a paper clip move in which of the following ways? S8P1c

    A. They vibrate.

    B. They vibrate and rotate.

    C. They vibrate, rotate and change positions (translate)

    D. They do not move.

53. The Law of Conservation of Matter S8P1g, 2a states that matter cannot be created or destroyed, but may change forms. The Law of Conservation of Energy states that energy cannot be created or destroyed, but it may change forms. From these two laws, we know that energy and mass are related. Which of the following important equations does not illustrate this mass-energy relationship?

    A. Snell's Law of refraction: $n_1 \sin\theta_1 = n_2 \sin\theta_2$

    B. The kinetic energy equation: $KE = \frac{1}{2}mv^2$

    C. The potential energy equation: $PE = mgh$

    D. Einstein's energy equation: $E = mc^2$

54. Which simple machine would be S8P3c useful for moving a box up 2 meters and to the right 3 meters?

    A. an inclined plane

    B. a screw

    C. a wedge

    D. a wheel and axel

55. After a chemical change takes place, S8P1e how can the products be returned to their original form?

    A. They cannot be changed back into the reactants.

    B. They can be changed back to the initial reactants through another chemical reaction.

    C. They can be changed back to the initial reactants through a physical process.

    D. They can be changed back to the initial reactants through a nuclear transformation.

56. Water (H_2O) is used to put out fires. S8P1d Hydrogen (H) and oxygen (O) are flammable gases. How do you explain this?

    A. The physical combination of hydrogen with oxygen changed the chemical property of flammability.

    B. The chemical combination of hydrogen with oxygen changed the chemical property of flammability.

    C. The physical combination of hydrogen with oxygen changed the physical property of flammability.

    D. The chemical combination of hydrogen with oxygen changed the physical property of flammability.

57. Different types of electromagnetic radiation have different characteristic wavelengths. ROY G BIV helps us remember the order of colors in the visible light portion of the electromagnetic spectrum. Red (R) has the longest wavelength and lowest energy, while violet (V) has the shortest wavelength and the highest energy. Another type of electromagnetic radiation is infrared, or "near red" radiation (IR). What can you infer about the relative wavelengths of visible and infrared radiation?   S8P4a, c

   A. It has a wavelength longer than red visible light.

   B. It has a wavelength that is the same as red visible light.

   C. It has a wavelength that is shorter than violet light.

   D. Infrared radiation has no energy.

58. Which of the following simple machines produces useful work with no thermal energy loss?   S8P3c

   A. inclined plane

   B. pulley

   C. both the inclined plane and the pulley

   D. neither the inclined plane or the pulley

59. Which of the following is not a wave?   S8P4a,5c

   A. X rays

   B. magnetic field lines

   C. visible light

   D. microwave radiation

60. Which of the following consist of atoms, rather than molecules?   S8P1a

   A. $LiCl(s)$

   B. $Cl_2(g)$

   C. $Li(s)$

   D. $HCl(g)$

A

acceleration 95, 97, 99, 105
  gravity 105
accuracy 40
alkali metal 65
alkaline earth metal 67
alternating current (AC) 119
ampere 121
amplitude 137, 140
analysis of error 49
atom 64
atomic mass 65
atomic number 65
average 46
average kinetic energy 91
average speed 96
average velocity 97

B

balances 36
bar graphs 45
base unit 38
batteries 123
bias data 26
Biomass 131
blue shift 141
bonding 67

C

cause and effect 30
Celsius 37
charts 44
chemical equation 75
chemical property 69
chemical reaction 67
circuit 123, 125
  parallel 124
  series 123
  switch 124
complex machine 111
compound 72
compounds 70, 75
conclusion 31, 48
conduction 92
conductor 121, 129
conductors 92
consensus 25
conservation of energy 85
control variables 31
convection 92
conversion factor 39
Coulomb's law 117
crests 137
current 129
current (I) 121

D

data 29, 44
data table 44
deceleration 97, 99

D (continued)

decibel 140
dependent variable 30, 45
descriptions of 102
diagram 43
diffraction 146
dimension 38
dimensional analysis 38
dimensional equation 39
direct current (DC) 119
displacement 95, 109
distance 95, 117
Doppler effect 141

E

efficient 112
electric field line 118
electric force 117
electrical current 121
electrical force 117
electrical potential 122
electricity, 121, 123
electromagnet 119
electromagnetic force 117, 119
electromagnetic induction 119
electromagnetic spectrum 138
electromagnetic wave 136
electrons 64
element symbol 65
elements 63
endothermic reaction 77
energy 129
  wave 140
ethics 24
exothermic reactions 77
explanation 47
extrapolation 45

F

Fahrenheit 37
families 65
fission 87
force 102
  types of 117
fossil fuels 131
frequency 137
friction 112
fulcrum 112
fusion 87

G

gases 81
generated 129
generator 129
Geothermal 132
graduated cylinder 36
grams 36
graphs 44
groups 65

H

halogens 67
heat 92
heterogeneous mixtures 71
homogeneous mixtures 71
hydroelectric power 130
hypothesis 30

I

inclined planes 111
independent variable 30, 45
inert 67
inertia 101
infer causes 54
inferences 47
input force 112
instantaneous velocity 96
insulators 92, 121
International System 36
ion 64

J

joule 110
journal 24

K

Kelvin 37
kinetic energy 85

L

law
    Coulomb's 117
    of gravity 105
Law of Conservation of Energy 77
Law of Conservation of Mass 75
lever 112
line graphs 45
lines of force 118
liquid 80
liters 36

M

machine 111
magazines 24
magnetic
    field 118
    field lines 118
magnetic force 117
mass 105, 117
masses 36
mean 46
mechanical advantage 112
mechanical efficiency 112
mechanical waves 135
median 46
medium 136
meniscus 36
metalloids 67

metals 65
meter stick 36
meters 36
metric prefix 38
metric system 38
mixtures 70, 71
mode 47
molecules 67, 72, 75

N

net force 104
neutrons 64
Newton
    universal law of gravity 105
Newton's First Law of Motion 101
noble gases 67
nonmetals 67
Nuclear Energy 87
Nuclear power 131
nucleus 64

O

observation 43
observe 30
Ohm's Law 122
ohmic devices 122
orbital 64
output force 112

P

peer review 24
Periodic Table 65
phase transition 81
phases 79
photovoltaic (solar) cell 132
physical property 69
potential energy 85
precision 40
predict outcomes 54
prediction 45
pressure 81
procedure 32
product 75
property 69
proportional 40
protons 64
pure substace 72
pyrophoric metal 76

Q

qualitative 43
quantitative 44

R

radiation 93, 136
rate 76, 129
ratio 40
reactants 75
red shift 141

research 30
resistance 122
resistors 123, 124, 126
risk-benefit analysis 27

S

scalars 95
science 23
scientific investigation 43
scientific process 31
scientists communicate 24
screws 111
semiconductors 67
series circuit 123
simple machine 111
solar power 132
solids 79
solution 71
sound wave 138
spectrum 141
speed 95, 96
states of matter 79
statistics 46
subjective 43
symbol 63

T

temperature 91
    measurement of 37
thermal energy 81, 92
thermal equilibrium 92
transformer 133
transition 85
transition metal 67
trends 45
troughs 137

U

U.S. Customary System 36

V

vacuum 136
variables 30, 45
vector diagrams 103
vectors 95, 103
velocity 95, 96
voltage 122, 125, 126
volts 122
volume 36

W

wave
    types of 138
wavelength 137, 141
wedge 111
weight 105
wind farms 130
wind power 130

PASSING THE

GEORGIA 8TH GRADE

CRCT IN SCIENCE

ANSWER KEY

July 2007

(Print 09/09)

American Book Company
PO Box 2638
Woodstock, GA 30188-1383
Toll Free: 1 (888) 264-5877 Phone: (770) 928-2834
Fax: (770) 928-7483 Toll Free Fax 1 (866) 827-3240
Web site: www.americanbookcompany.com

8th Grade Georgia Science
Standards Chart

Passing the Georgia 8th Grade CRCT in Science

Chart of Standards

The following chart correlates each question on the Diagnostic Test, Practice Test 1, and Practice Test 2 to the 8th grade science *standards published by the Georgia Department of Education*. These test questions are also correlated with chapters in *Passing the Georgia 8th Grade CRCT in Science*

Content Goal	Chapter Number	Diagnostic Test Questions	Practice Test 1 Questions	Practice Test 2 Questions
S8P1: Students will examine the scientific view of the nature of matter.				
a. Distinguish between atoms and molecules.	6	48	35, 41, 55	49, 60
b. Describe the difference between pure substances (elements and compounds) and mixtures.	7	48	9, 26	26, 28
c. Describe the movement of particles in solids, liquids, gasses and plasmas states.	9	17, 29, 51, 53	17, 51	26, 40, 46, 52
d. Distinguish between physical and chemical properties of matter as physical (i.e., density, melting point, boiling point) or chemical (i.e., reactivity, combustibility).	7	3, 7, 18, 30, 40, 52, 60	3, 12, 15, 28, 31, 36, 41	1, 2, 18, 56

Content Goal	Chapter Number	Diagnostic Test Questions	Practice Test 1 Questions	Practice Test 2 Questions
e. Distinguish between changes in matter as physical (e.e., physical change) or chemical (development of a gas, formation of precipitate, and change in color).	7	4, 7, 12, 36, 43	2, 18, 26	3, 7, 11, 17, 25, 40,46, 55
f. Recognize that there are more than 100 elements and some have similar properties as shown on the Periodic Table of Elements.	6	11, 44, 56	4, 14, 32	9, 24
g. Identify and demonstrate the Law of Conservation of Matter.	8	14	8, 52	30, 53
S8P2: Students will be familiar with the forms and transformation of energy.				
a. Explain energy transformation in terms of the Law of Conservation of Energy.	10, 17	58		33, 36, 53
b. Explain the relationship between potential and kinetic energy.	10	38	7, 29, 38, 48	10, 32
c. Compare and contrast the different forms of energy (heat, light, electricity, mechanical motion, sound) and their characteristics.	10, 17	6	23, 44, 46	4, 32, 33

Content Goal	Chapter Number	Diagnostic Test Questions	Practice Test 1 Questions	Practice Test 2 Questions
d. Describe how heat can be transferred through matter by collisions of atoms (conduction) or through space (radiation). In a liquid or gas, currents will facilitate the transfer of heat (convection).	11	34, 45, 50	17, 19, 22, 44, 45	13, 14, 29,36
S8P3: Students will investigate relationships between force, mass and the motion of objects.				
a. Determine the relationship between velocity and acceleration.	12	5, 23, 46	6, 37, 47	23, 34, 43
b. Demonstrate the effects of balanced and unbalanced forces on an object in terms of gravity, inertia, and friction.	13	1, 42, 47	5, 6, 10, 37, 58	12, 16, 23
c. Demonstrate the effects of simple machines (lever, inclined plane, pulley, wedgy, screw, and wheel and axel) on work.	14	2, 13, 16, 21	1, 58	16, 38, 47, 54, 58

Content Goal	Chapter Number	Diagnostic Test Questions	Practice Test 1 Questions	Practice Test 2 Questions
S8P4: Students will explore the wave nature of sound and electromagnetic radiation.				
a. Identify the characteristics of electromagnetic and mechanical waves.	18	31, 32	27, 50, 57	37, 45, 57, 59
b. Describe how the behavior of light waves is manipulated causing reflecting, refraction diffraction and absorption.	19	27, 39, 41, 55	13, 20, 24, 25	6, 15, 50
c. Explain how the human eye sees objects and colors in terms of wavelengths.	19	39, 59	25, 56	37, 57
d. Describe how the behavior of waves is affected by medium (such as air, water, solids).	18	28, 54	13, 24, 50	6, 15, 35
e. Relate the properties of sound to everyday experiments.	18	32, 54	30	44, 48
f. Diagram the parts of the wave and explain how the parts are affected by changes in amplitude and pitch.	18	10, 35	53	45, 48

Content Goal	Chapter Number	Diagnostic Test Questions	Practice Test 1 Questions	Practice Test 2 Questions
S8P5: Students will recognize characteristics of gravity, electricity, and magnetism as major kinds of forces acting in nature.				
a. Recognize that every objects exerts gravitational force on every other object and that the force exerted depends on how much mass the objects have and how far apart they are.	13	19	39, 49, 60	51
b. Demonstrate the advantages and disadvantages of series and parallel circuits and how they transfer energy.	16, 17	26	38, 54	22, 41
c. Investigate and explain that electric currents and magnets can exert force on each other.	15	25, 33, 49	33, 39, 40, 49, 59	31, 59

S8CS1: Student will explore the importance of curiosity, honesty, openness, and skepticism in science and will exhibit these traits in their own efforts to understand how the world works.				
a. Understand the importance of — and keep— honest, clear and accurate records in science.	1			
b. Understand that hypotheses can be valuable even if they turn out not to be completely accurate.	2			
S8CS2: Students will use standard safety practices for all classroom laboratory and field investigations.				
a. Follow correct procedures for use of scientific apparatus.	5	37	2	5, 42
b. Demonstrate appropriate techniques in all laboratory situations.	5		42	2, 5, 8, 19, 42
c. Follow correct protocol for identifying and reporting safety problems and violations.	5		42	5

S8CS3: Students will have the computation and estimation skills necessary for analyzing data and following scientific explanations.				
a. Analyze scientific data by using, interpreting, and comparing number in several equivalent forms, such as integers, fractions, decimals and percents.	3			21
b. Find the mean, median and mode and use them to analyze a set of scientific data.	4	57	21	
c. Apply the metric system to scientific investigations that include metric and metric conversions (i.e., centimeters to meters).	3	24		
d. Decide what degree of precision is adequate, and round off appropriately.	3	15, 24	34	
e. Address the relationship between accuracy and precision.	3			
f. Use ratios and proportions, including constant rates, in appropriate problems.	3			43, 44

Contain Goal	Chapter Number	Diagnostic Test Questions	Practice Test 1 Questions	Practice Test 2 Questions
S8CS4: Students will use tools and instruments for observing, measuring, and manipulating equipment and materials in scientific activities utilizing safe laboratory procedures.				
a. Use appropriate technology to store and retrieve scientific information in topical, alphabetical, numerical, and keyword files, and create simple files.	4			
b. Use appropriate tools and unites for measuring objects and/or substances.	3	20	43	20
c. Learn and use standard safety practices when conducting scientific investigations.	5		11, 16	5
S8CS5: Students will use the ideas of system, model, change, and scale in exploring scientific and technological matters.				
a. Observe and explain how parts can be related to other parts in a system such as the role of simple machine in complex machines.	4			
b. Understand that different models (such as physical replicas, pictures, and analogies) can be used to represent the same thing.	4			

Content Goal	Chapter Number	Diagnostic Test Questions	Practice Test 1 Questions	Practice Test 2 Questions
S8CS6: Students will communicate scientific ideas and activities clearly.				
a. Write clear, step-by-step instructions for conducting scientific investigations, operating a piece of equipment or following a procedure.	2			
b. Write for scientific purposes incorporating information from a circle, bar or line graph, data tables, diagrams and symbols.	4			37
c. Organize scientific information in appropriate tables, charts and graphs, and identify relationships they reveal.	4	22	14	1

Content Goal	Chapter Number	Diagnostic Test Questions	Practice Test 1 Questions	Practice Test 2 Questions
S8CS7: Students will question scientific claims and arguments effectively.				
a. Question claims based on vague attributions (such as "Leading doctors say...") or on statements made by people outside the area of their particular expertise.	1			
b. Identify the flaws of reasoning in arguments that are based on poorly designed research (e.g., facts intermingled with opinion, conclusion based on insufficient evidence).	1	8		27, 39
c. Question the value of arguments based on small samples of data, biased samples or samples for which there was no control.	1			
d. Recognize that there may be more than one way to interpret a given set of findings.	1	7		

Content Goal	Chapter Number	Diagnostic Test Questions	Practice Test 1 Questions	Practice Test 2 Questions
S8CS8: Students will be familiar with the characteristics of scientific knowledge and how it is achieved. Students will apply the following to scientific concepts:				
a. When similar investigations give different results, the scientific challenge is to judge whether the differences are trivial or significant, which often requires further study.				39
b. When new experimental results are inconsistent with an existing, well-established theory, scientist may pursue further experimentation to determine whether the results are flawed or the theory requires modification.				
c. As prevailing theories are challenged by new information, scientific knowledge may change.				

Content Goal	Chapter Number	Diagnostic Test Questions	Practice Test 1 Questions	Practice Test 2 Questions
S8CS9: Students will understand the features of the process of scientific inquiry.				
a. Investigations are conducted for different reasons, which include exploring new phenomena, confirming previous results, testing how well a theory predicts, and comparing different theories. Scientific investigations usually involve collecting evidence, reasoning, devising hypotheses, and formulating explanations to make sense of collected evidence.	2	3		
b. Scientific investigation usually involve collecting evidence, reasoning, devising hypotheses, and formulating explanations to make sense of collected evidence.	2		15	
c. Scientific experiments investigate the effect of one variable on another. All other variables are kept constant.	2	9		
d. Scientists often collaborate to design research. To prevent this bias, scientists conduct independent studies of the same questions.	1			

Content Goal	Chapter Number	Diagnostic Test Questions	Practice Test 1 Questions	Practice Test 2 Questions
e. Accurate record keeping, data sharing, and replication of results are essential for maintaining an investigator's credibility with other scientists and society.	1	9		
f. Scientists use technology and mathematics to enhance the process of scientific inquiry.	3		.	
g. The ethics of science require that special care must be taken and used for human subjects and animals in scientific research. Scientist must adhere to the appropriate rules and guidelines when conducting research.	2			
S9CS10: Students will enhance reading in all curriculum areas by:				
a. Reading in all curriculum areas.				4, 39
b. Discussing books				
c. Building vocabulary knowledge				3, 25
d. Establishing context				

ANSWER KEY

Diagnostic Test

Pages 1–17

1. B	11. A	21. D	31. D	41. B	51. A
2. A	12. A	22. B	32. A	42. A	52. A
3. A	13. D	23. D	33. B	43. B	53. B
4. C	14. C	24. C	34. B	44. B	54. C
5. A	15. C	25. A	35. D	45. C	55. D
6. A	16. B	26. B	36. D	46. C	56. A
7. B	17. B	27. B	37. D	47. D	57. A
8. C	18. B	28. B	38. C	48. B	58. B
9. B	19. A	29. C	39. A	49. C	59. C
10. D	20. B	30. A	40. B	50. A	60. C

Chapter 1: What is Science?

Chapter 1 Review

Page 28

1. C	2. C	3. C	4. B	5. B

Chapter 2: The Basic Method

Chapter 2 Review

Page 34

1. B	2. D	3. C	4. D	5. B

Chapter 3: Equipment and Measurements

Practice Exercise

Page 41

The second thermometer would give a more precise temperature reading because it measures to the nearest 1 degree. The first thermometer only measures to the nearest 5 degrees.

Chapter 3 Review

Page 42

1. A   2. A   3. B   4. D   5. A

Chapter 4: Data and Its Presentation

Challenge Activity

Page 48

2. observation: man is on the phone

inference: the man is very busy

3. observation: the person is walking the dog

inference: it is cold outside

4. observation: the person is laying in bed.

inference: the person is sick

5. observation: the person is in a laboratory

inference: the person is smart

6. observation: the child is feeding the dolphin a fish

inference the boy is friends with the dolphin.

Chapter 4 Review

Page 50

1. C   2. D   3. B   4. C   5. D

Chapter 5: Laboratory Safety

Scavenger Hunt

Page 53

Figure 1.2 shows a girl conducting laboratory work without her safety goggles. She should put them on!

Think while you work

Page 54

1. 20°C was the starting temp, about room temperature.

2. At 12 min., a prediction around 100°C would be acceptable

3. No, he should use tongs or heat-resistant mitts.

4. Since Rodrigo is boiling water, he does not need a mask. But he should be wearing goggles to protect his eyes.

Challenge Activity

Page 55 (top)

1. In a chemical fumehood.

2. At 60 seconds, a prediction just over 6 grams would be acceptable.

3. The mass lost was the mass associated with fume matter.

Challenge Activity

Page 55 (bottom)

1. Broken glass

2. Ray, Tim and Lou are roughhousing; Ann has open-toed shoes; Bob has broken glass; everyone, except Tina and Carl, is not wearing goggles; Sue has dangling hair and jewelry; Joe Lou, Jim, Luke and Duke are using equipment improperly.

3. Accept any possible graph

4. Accept reasonable responses.

Chapter 5 Review

Page 56

| 1. A | 2. A | 3. A | 4. C | 5. C |

Unit 1 Review

Pages 57–59

1. D	4. B	7. B*	10. C
2. D	5. B	8. A	11. D
3. C	6. B	9. A	

* B is the correct answer, but the number of students who answer C should generate class discussion on the precision of the thermometer.

Unit 2: Physical Science

Chapter 6: Atoms and Elements

Chapter 6 Review

Page 68

| 1. D | 2. A | 3. A | 4. C | 5. A |

Vocabulary Builder

Chalcogens (with the "ch" pronounced as a hard "c", like in chemistry) are Group 16. They are also known as the oxygen group.

Pnicogens (pronounced ni-ke-jen) is the name for Group 15 of the Periodic Table. They are also known as the nitrogen group. Teachers may use this old fashioned name to help students remember the two most prominent elements in the Group: phosphorous (P) and nitrogen (N).

Chapter 7: Properties of Matter

Chapter 7 Review

Page 74

| 1. A | 2. D | 3. C | 4. B | 5. B |

Chapter 8: Chemical Reactions

Challenge Question

Page 75

The law of conservation of mass tells you that you would have the same mass of products as reactants, even if they are in different chemical formations. So, the reactant mass was 10 grams.

Chapter 8 Review

Page 78

1. B   2. C   3. C   4. C   5. A

Chapter 9: States of Matter

Challenge Question
Page 80
Melting Point
Challenge Question
Page 80
Boiling Point
Challenge Activity
Page 82
As steam is cooled, the movement of gaseous water atoms (remember, this is recorded as its temperature) will decrease. When the gas reaches 100° C, more energy will be lost from the gas phase as the attractive forces between atoms reforms. Just like before, though, the temperature remains constant during the transition (the flat part of the graph). Finally, when condensation (gas turning into a liquid) is complete, the temperature of the liquid will begin to fall, as energy is withdrawn.

Activity: Phase Transitions
Page 83

condensation

precipitation

sublimation

melting

evaporation

deposition

Chapter 9 Review

Page 84

1. A   2. C   3. B   4. D   5. D

Vocabulary Builder
Page 84
Vibrate - to move side to side, oscillate.
Rotate - to move in a circular path around an axis.
Translate - to move from one point to another in linear motion.
The common definition of translate is to transform a passage written in one language into an equivalent passage in another
    language. When we discuss translation as a mode of motion, we are talking about something moving from one place to another
    place. In both cases, we describe a path of progress: from one place or language to another place or language.

Chapter 10: Energy

Activity
Page 89
chemical to mechanical
several answers are possible — nuclear to radiant to chemical is inferred although nuclear may be left off.
chemical to mechanical
electrical to thermal

Activity
Page 89
1. The corn stalk is converting the radiant energy of the Sun into the chemical energy of photosynthesis. The student may also note that the chemical energy of photosynthesis is converted to mechanical energy of explosive (for a plant) physical growth.)

2. The candle wick is made of some flammable material. The chemical energy in the material is converted to the radiant and thermal energy of fire.)

3. The solar cell converts the radiant energy of the Sun into electrical energy, which powers the rovers. The student should understand that the solar cell does not turn the thermal energy from the Sun into electricity (although thermal energy is a by-product of the radiant to electrical energy transition).

4. In the Sun, nuclear energy is converted to radiant and thermal energy. (The student may note that, since new products are formed from the process of fusing atoms, chemical and nuclear energy is also a byproduct.)

5. Tanya's voice consists of sound waves. The telephone converts the sound waves to an electrical impulse which is transmitted to Olivia's phone. There it is converted back into sound waves. So this is an example of sound energy transforming into electrical energy and then back into sound energy.)

Chapter 10 Review

Page 90
1. B   2. D   3. C   4. D   5. A

Vocabulary Builder
Page 90
Think of two particles, about to collide (run into each other). An elastic collision is one in which all kinetic energy of the moving particles before the collision is the same as their kinetic energy after the collision. When atoms or molecules in a gas collide, they are elastic collisions. When objects like balls or cars collide, collisions are not elastic, as energy is lost to friction and heat.

Chapter 11: Thermal Energy

Challenge Question
Page 92
The cold of the can absorbs energy in the form of heat from the water droplets in surrounding air. Condensation is the result.

Chapter 11 Review

Page 94
1. C   2. B   3. C   4. A   5. D

Chapter 12: Velocity and Acceleration

Challenge Question
Page 99
For the average velocity to be 6 m/s, the instantaneous velocity must have been higher at some point. It could be that the instantaneous velocity was 2 m/s @ 0.1s, 10/ m/s @ 0.5s, then slowed to 6 m/s @ 0.9 seconds.

Chapter 12 Review

Page 100
1. D   2. C   3. B   4. B   5. A

Chapter 13: Forces and Motion
Activity
Page 106
1. student should indicate a net force of 350N with a right-pointing arrow.
2. may draw either way, but the net force of 2N should be pointing in the direction Johnny is pushing.
3. Students should indicate in drawing (1) and upward arrow (normal force) equal in magnitude to a downward arrow (gravity), net force is zero. For (2), a downward arrow represents gravity and is only opposed by a very small upward arrow, which represents the frictional force of air resistance. For (3) the drawing will look the same as (1). (1) &(3) look the same because, in both scenarios, Marylynn is not moving, therefore, the force acting on her are balanced.

Challenge Activity
Page 107
1. F1 = gravitational force, F2 = normal force, F3 = applied force and F4 = frictional force.
2. -9.81N
3. The student should realize that any direction that a book is pushed will involve an oppositional frictional force. A force must be applied that is larger than the frictional force. If the book is to move to the left, then F4 must be greater than the F3.
4. The normal force is a balanced force that opposes gravity. It will not spontaneously increase to overcome the downward force of gravity. In order for the book to move upward, some upward force must be applied to it. The student may choose to draw a new arrow upward (F5) that is larger than the existing F1.

Chapter 13 Review
Page 108

1. A	2. C	3. D	4. A	5. C

Chapter 14: Work
Chapter 14 Review
Page 116

1. A	2. C	3. A	4. B	5. B

Chapter 15: Electromagnetic Force
Chapter 15 Review
Page 120

1. D	2. D	3. A	4. A	5. B

Chapter 16: Electrical Circuits
Challenge Question 1
Page 124
Figure 16.6 $R_{EQ} = 6\,\Omega$
Figure 16.6 $R_{EQ} =$ infinity - no current will flow

Challenge Question 2
Page 124
$V_{EQ} = 1.5 + 1.5 = 3V$
Challenge Question 3
Page 125
Figure 16.10 V_{EQ} - 1.5V

Practice Exercise: Series and Parallel Circuits
Page 126
1.

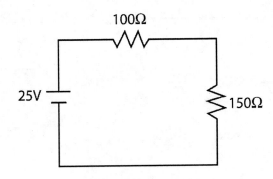

$R_{EQ} = 100\ \Omega + 150\Omega = 250\Omega$
$I = \underline{V} = 25V/250\Omega = 0.10A$
$ R$

2.

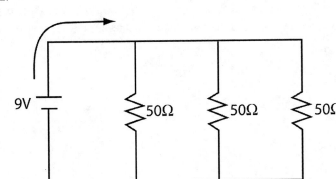

$$\frac{1}{R_{EQ}} = \frac{1}{50} + \frac{1}{50} + \frac{1}{50}$$

$$\frac{1}{R_{EQ}} = \frac{3}{50} \quad \text{and} \quad R_{EQ} = \frac{50}{3}$$

$$I = \frac{9V}{50/(3\Omega)}$$

$$I = 9V\left(\frac{3}{50}\right)\Omega = 0.54A$$

3.

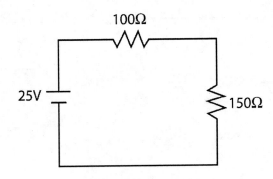

$R_{EQ} = R_1 + R_2 + R_3 + R_4 + R_5$

NOTE: The student may also draw the circuit with an open switch between R_4 and R_5.

7

4.

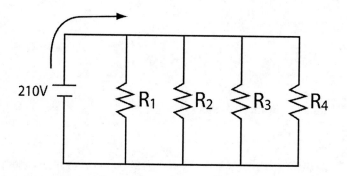

$$\frac{1}{R_{EQ}} = \frac{1}{R_1} + \frac{1}{R_2} + \frac{1}{R_3} + \frac{1}{R_4}$$

NOTE: The student may also draw the circuit with an open switch on the R_4 loop.

Challenge Activity
Page 127
A. series   B. parallel   C. series   D. parallel   E. series   F. parallel
Challenge Activity
Page 127

Rearranging Ohm's Law to fit the parameters in the challenge activity gives you : $I = \frac{V}{R}$.

Emphasize to your students that this can be correlated to the standard graphing equation y = ms. Doing that, they should quickly realize that the slope m will be $\frac{1}{R}$. Graphing this results in an arc starting at the origin, bending out, the levelling off.

Chapter 16 Review
Page 128
1. B   2. B   3. A   4. C   5. A

Chapter 17: Electricity in Our Lives
Challenge Question
Page 130
Flowing water: kinetic. Dammed water: potential. Water pushing the generator is moving, so its energy can be described as kinetic.
Chapter 17 Review
Page 134
1. A   2. D   3. B   4. C   5. B

Chapter 18: Properties of Waves
Chapter 18 Review
Page 142
1. C   2. C   3. A   4. A   5. B

Chapter 19: Behavior of Waves
Chapter 19 Review
Page 148
1. B   2. C   3. B   4. B   5. A

Unit 2 Review
Pages 149 –152

1. C	3. B	5. D	7. A	9. A	11. A	13. C	15. C	17. C	19. A
2. A	4. D	6. B	8. D	10. D	12. A	14. A	16. D	18. B	20. A

Post Test 1
Pages 153–168

1. A	11. C	21. D	31. A	41. A	51. C
2. B	12. D	22. B	32. A	42. C	52. B
3. B	13. C	23. D	33. C	43. D	53. C
4. A	14. B	24. C	34. B	44. D	54. D
5. A	15. C	25. A	35. A	45. D	55. C
6. D	16. C	26. A	36. B	46. C	56. C
7. D	17. A	27. B	37. C	47. B	57. A
8. A	18. B	28. C	38. C	48. D	58. C
9. A	19. C	29. B	39. B	49. A	59. D
10. B	20. B	30. C	40. D	50. A	60. B

Post Test 2
Pages 169–184

1. C	11. C	21. B	31. B	41. A	51. C
2. B	12. A	22. A	32. A	42. A	52. A
3. B	13. A	23. B	33. D	43. C	53. A
4. B	14. B	24. C	34. D	44. D	54. A
5. C	15. A	25. A	35. A	45. D	55. B
6. D	16. D	26. C	36. C	46. D	56. B
7. B	17. C	27. C	37. C	47. C	57. A
8. B	18. B	28. C	38. C	48. A	58. D
9. C	19. B	29. A	39. C	49. C	59. B
10. C	20. C	30. C	40. B	50. D	60. C

American Book Company
The Standards Experts

CRCT

Please fill out the form completely, and return by mail or fax to American Book Company.

Purchase Order #: _____ Date: _____ Contact Person: _____

School Name (and District, if any): _____ Phone: _____ Fax: _____

_____ E-mail: _____

Credit Card #: _____ Exp. Date: _____ Authorized Signature: _____

Billing Address: _____ Shipping Address: _____

Attn: _____ ☐ same as billing Attn: _____

Order Number	Product Title	Pricing* (10 books)	Qty	Pricing (30 books)	Qty	Pricing (30 e-books)	Qty	Pricing (30 books+e-books)	Qty	To
GA6-L0508	Mastering the Georgia 6th Grade CRCT in ELA	$169.90 (1 set of 10 books)		$329.70 (1 set of 30 books)		$329.70 (1 set of 30 books)		$599.40 (30 books+30 e-books)		
GA6-M0305	Mastering the Georgia 6th Grade CRCT in Math	$169.90 (1 set of 10 books)		$329.70 (1 set of 30 books)		$329.70 (1 set of 30 books)		$599.40 (30 books+30 e-books)		
GA6-R0108	Mastering the Georgia 6th Grade CRCT in Reading	$169.90 (1 set of 10 books)		$329.70 (1 set of 30 books)		$329.70 (1 set of 30 books)		$599.40 (30 books+30 e-books)		
GA6-S1206	Mastering the Georgia 6th Grade CRCT in Science	$169.90 (1 set of 10 books)		$329.70 (1 set of 30 books)		$329.70 (1 set of 30 books)		$599.40 (30 books+30 e-books)		
GA6-H0208	Mastering the Georgia 6th Grade CRCT in Social Studies	$169.90 (1 set of 10 books)		$329.70 (1 set of 30 books)		$329.70 (1 set of 30 books)		$599.40 (30 books+30 e-books)		
GA7-L0508	Mastering the Georgia 7th Grade CRCT in ELA	$169.90 (1 set of 10 books)		$329.70 (1 set of 30 books)		$329.70 (1 set of 30 books)		$599.40 (30 books+30 e-books)		
GA7-M0305	Mastering the Georgia 7th Grade CRCT in Math	$169.90 (1 set of 10 books)		$329.70 (1 set of 30 books)		$329.70 (1 set of 30 books)		$599.40 (30 books+30 e-books)		
GA7-R0707	Mastering the Georgia 7th Grade CRCT in Reading	$169.90 (1 set of 10 books)		$329.70 (1 set of 30 books)		$329.70 (1 set of 30 books)		$599.40 (30 books+30 e-books)		
GA7-S1206	Mastering the Georgia 7th Grade CRCT in Science	$169.90 (1 set of 10 books)		$329.70 (1 set of 30 books)		$329.70 (1 set of 30 books)		$599.40 (30 books+30 e-books)		
GA7-H0208	Mastering the Georgia 7th Grade CRCT in Social Studies	$169.90 (1 set of 10 books)		$329.70 (1 set of 30 books)		$329.70 (1 set of 30 books)		$599.40 (30 books+30 e-books)		
GA8-L0505	Passing the Georgia 8th Grade CRCT in ELA	$169.90 (1 set of 10 books)		$329.70 (1 set of 30 books)		$329.70 (1 set of 30 books)		$599.40 (30 books+30 e-books)		
GA8-MATH08	Passing the Georgia 8th Grade CRCT in Math	$169.90 (1 set of 10 books)		$329.70 (1 set of 30 books)		$329.70 (1 set of 30 books)		$599.40 (30 books+30 e-books)		
GA8-R0505	Passing the Georgia 8th Grade CRCT in Reading	$169.90 (1 set of 10 books)		$329.70 (1 set of 30 books)		$329.70 (1 set of 30 books)		$599.40 (30 books+30 e-books)		
GA8-S0707	Passing the Georgia 8th Grade CRCT in Science	$169.90 (1 set of 10 books)		$329.70 (1 set of 30 books)		$329.70 (1 set of 30 books)		$599.40 (30 books+30 e-books)		
GA8-H0607	Passing the Georgia 8th Grade CRCT in Georgia Studies	$169.90 (1 set of 10 books)		$329.70 (1 set of 30 books)		$329.70 (1 set of 30 books)		$599.40 (30 books+30 e-books)		
GA8-HS0710	Passing the Georgia 8th Grade CRCT in Georgia Studies Studies	$169.90 (1 set of 10 books)		$329.70 (1 set of 30 books)		$329.70 (1 set of 30 books)		$599.40 (30 books+30 e-books)		
GA8-W0907	Passing the Georgia Grade 8 Writing Assessment	$169.90 (1 set of 10 books)		$329.70 (1 set of 30 books)		$329.70 (1 set of 30 books)		$599.40 (30 books+30 e-books)		

-1-11   *Minimum order is 1 set of 10 books of the same subject.

Subtotal

Shipping & Handling 12%
Shipping 6% on print and digital packages
Shipping waived on digital resources.

Total

American Book Company ● PO Box 2638 ● Woodstock, GA 30188-1383
Toll Free Phone: 1-888-264-5877 ● Toll-Free Fax: 1-866-827-3240
Web Site: www.americanbookcompany.com

Call Toll-Free 1-888-264-5877 to ORDER and for FREE PREVIEW COPIE